D0160439

Hail to the CEO

The Failure of George W. Bush and the Cult of Moral Leadership

James Hoopes

PRAEGER

Westport, Connecticut
London

Library of Congress Cataloging-in-Publication Data

Hoopes, James, 1944–

Hail to the CEO : the failure of George W. Bush and the cult of moral leadership / James Hoopes.

   p. cm.

Includes bibliographical references and index.

ISBN 978-0-313-34784-9 (alk. paper)

1. Bush, George W. (George Walker), 1946– —Ethics. 2. Bush, George W. (George Walker), 1946– —Political and social views. 3. Political leadership—United States—Case studies. 4. Business and politics—United States—Case studies. 5. Political ethics—United States—Case studies. 6. United States—Politics and government—2001– 7. Political corruption—United States. 8. United States—Moral conditions. 9. Presidents—United States—Biography. I. Title.

E903.3.H66   2008

973.931092—dc22   2007035414

British Library Cataloguing in Publication Data is available.

Library of Congress Catalog Card Number: 2007035414

ISBN: 978-0-313-34784-9

First published in 2008

Praeger Publishers, 88 Post Road West, Westport, CT 06881

An imprint of Greenwood Publishing Group, Inc.

www.praeger.com

Printed in the United States of America

∞™

The paper used in this book complies with the Permanent Paper Standard issued by the National Information Standards Organization (Z39.48–1984).

10 9 8 7 6 5 4 3 2 1

In memory of Marty Tropp

Contents

Introduction

We have a dearth of honest sachems and a raft of charlatan chiefs. Throughout society—in government, business, and non-profits—too many of our leaders are long on moral talk and short on moral action. George W. Bush, touting values he violates, embodies and exemplifies our crisis of moral leadership.

Sometimes honest, sometimes not, Bush probably falls somewhere in the middle range of humanity's sad record on integrity. In arrogance and brashness he is high on the chart. Yet he thinks of himself as a moral leader.

Bush is not alone. Many business leaders believe that pre-eminence is a mark of purity. The idea that leaders are models of morality is so widespread in corporate life as to amount to a cult.

The cult of moral leadership holds that leaders, like cream, rise by their sublimity. But this idea of leaders as moral exemplars can encourage morally corrosive false pride. We have a spate of dishonest leaders not in spite of but at least partly because of widespread confidence that leadership is intrinsically moral when in fact it is morally dangerous.

The cult of moral leadership deepens that danger by disguising it. By giving leaders false moral confidence, the leadership cult destroys their moral caution, making them more likely to slip into wrongdoing. Sublime on the surface, the leadership cult is corrupt at the core.

The more democratic and more realistic idea is that a position of leadership imperils the character. Democratic tradition holds that power corrupts and that its possessors must therefore be fenced in by checks and balances. The leadership cult endangers democracy by causing leaders, and followers as well, to forget that power has no claim on our trust.

Often implied rather than explicitly stated, the idea that leaders are or should be moral paragons has gone largely unnoticed. So has its threat to democracy. Many citizens who pride themselves on being up to date on social and political issues are unaware that there is an undemocratic cult loose in the land.

Genuinely moral leadership depends on a paradox. Only those who recognize that they may be or become morally unfit to lead are morally worthy to do so. People confident of their purity are morally unqualified to lead.

The popular idea of "managing by values" is a corollary of the leadership cult. The idea—true as far as it goes—is that we act according to our values. Therefore companies adopt values statements, ethics codes, corporate credos, and the like to inspire employees to do the right thing.

But a company's idea of what it values can easily be wrong. Traditional religion and modern psychology agree that the human heart often deceives itself. How, then, can a company—or for that matter a country—composed of many human beings be certain of what it values?

Leaders should therefore manage *for* values, not *by* them. Instead of pretending to know what the company values, leaders should state what they want the company to value. They should say to employees: "Here are our values goals. Act in a way that helps achieve these goals."

Treating values as goals is consistent with the way character building really works. The great philosopher Aristotle said that virtue is a "habit" to be acquired through repeated action. According to Aristotle, we become just people "by doing just acts."

Our personal experience confirms Aristotle's wisdom in thinking of virtue as a "habit" developed through practice. For example, if we passed up an opportunity to cheat in school, we found it easier to do the right thing the next time the situation arose. And sadly, personal experience teaches that just saying we have good values does not mean we will always act right.

The danger of putting words before deeds is why companies should not issue lofty values statements. As Aristotle saw, our actions, not our words, establish our values. Companies that state their values as if they are a done deal run the risk of slipping into moral complacency if not moral arrogance.

This book therefore aims to help leaders by showing that genuinely moral leadership requires treating values as goals, not tools. It requires managing *for* values, not *by* them. To manage *by* values risks treating values as means to an end. To manage *for* values is to treat values as ends in themselves.

For followers, this book reveals the telltale signs that distinguish feckless and phony leaders from honest and effective ones. The former believe in their inspirational qualities and think that leadership is mainly a matter of managing by values. Good leaders do the hard work of using their power to manage for values, thereby earning moral influence and winning followers.

For citizens, this book warns that it would be wrong to sigh with relief when George Bush leaves the Oval Office. If his successor is a person of some decency and good values, those qualities will be no more a guarantee against moral mistakes than they were in Bush. Undemocratic notions of moral leadership are so appealing to people of power that we will always have to be on guard against them in our political leaders.

This book can scarcely prove that Bush subscribes to the leadership cult. No available record shows him converting to the cult of moral leadership in the way that, for example, his religious conversion has been documented. Only circumstantial evidence—such as his frequent attempts to lead by values—supports the idea that he adheres to the cult of moral leadership.

But whether or not Bush is a disciple of the leadership cult, he often acts as if he is. As this book shows, he often tries to use values to lead. Regardless, therefore, of the degree to which he is actually influenced by the leadership cult, its dangers are illustrated by his many mistakes.

To say that a person has made mistakes is no necessary reflection on his or her underlying qualities. We find this distinction between the quality of a person's actions and the quality of his or her character harder to accept in the moral sphere than in the physical world. It is no insult to an athlete's talent to say that in one part of his game he has a bad technique that leads to mistakes. But in moral life, which comes so much closer to the heart of who we are and want to be, it is harder to acknowledge a person's errors without assuming that it reflects on his character rather than, for example, mistaken techniques of leadership.

It would have been impossible to write this book without making some judgments as to good and bad qualities in Bush's character. The interplay of his character and his attempts to manage by values have helped make him, as I see it, one of our worst presidents. But this book's main argument is that the leadership cult can be morally dangerous to people who want to do well. It is not my purpose to pass any overall judgment on Bush's moral standing as a human being.

To the extent that I do judge Bush's character and intentions, I attempt as much as the evidence will permit to decide in his favor. My argument as to the moral danger of the leadership cult is strengthened, not weakened, by acknowledging that Bush, like the rest of fallen humanity, has his good points. It is because it can take more than good values to do the right thing that the ethical errors in the leadership cult pose a moral danger to those who believe in it or, as in Bush's case, act as if they believe in it.

Of course, many ideas other than the leadership cult are morally dangerous to American leaders. The old idea of the United States as a redeemer nation with a providential role to play in history has been augmented by recent developments. Triumphant capitalists in the world's only superpower are tempted to view the defeat of communism as a reflection on their personal virtue. Neoconservative ideologues overestimate their, and the world's, moral clarity. And some people of faith profess their piety with impious self-righteousness.

The movement of morally arrogant leadership from business to government is not uniquely American. Anywhere in the world, the tyrant of tomorrow is as likely to wear a suit and tie as epaulets and a sidearm. Chief executive officers (CEOs) even more than generalissimos can claim the prowess to make the trains run on time.

Yet America is at special risk from the leadership cult because of its extraordinary power and because of the fact that the new global culture—corporate culture—is most highly developed in the United States. Modern corporate management is an American invention. It is because American business has had more practice that it leads the world in rationalizing undemocratic managerial power with mistaken theories of moral leadership.

Self-appointed moral leaders in the business world are too often blind to the dangers that threaten their characters. Guided by the leadership cult, they may see no reflection on themselves when their colleagues are hauled off to jail. It is no reason for surprise that the business world had hardly begun to recover from Enron, WorldCom, and dozens of other accounting scandals before there was a new wave of corporate criminality around backdated options.

All too often, leaders who sincerely believe in their virtue are actually corrupt. Hoary platitudes attributing such moral self-delusion to the temptations of power are correct but often incomplete explanations. The leadership cult also helps leaders hide their wrongdoing from themselves.

Worse, the leadership cult has spread from business to non-profits and government. Churches, charities, foundations, hospitals, universities, local school committees, town halls, and state capitols are increasingly infested with ethically naive, self-appointed moral leaders. There is no reason to suppose that our national government or democracy in general is exempt from the moral dangers of the leadership cult.

The leadership cult endangers executives not only morally but also practically by encouraging them to devalue competence and knowledge. Trying to use values to lead, executives may be tempted to substitute values and vision for hands-on management. Operation Iraqi Freedom and Hurricane Katrina have brought home all too clearly that putatively moral leadership cannot replace managerial competence and know-how.

A case can be made for many of Bush's presidential policies, but his most defensible initiatives have required the least leadership. His education bill, for example, enjoyed widespread support that made its enactment easy. Where leadership was more difficult, Bush has far too often been on the wrong side.

Chapters 6 through 8 show that during Bush's presidency some of his worst failures of leadership came from trying to use values to lead. By trying to use moral influence rather than a strong legislative program to deal with corporate corruption, he forfeited control of the post-Enron movement for business reform, opening the way for heavy government regulation that he had hoped to avoid. By offering government funding to faith-based initiatives, he undermined the religious spirit he meant to support. With his one-man declaration of war on terror, he violated the Constitution he had sworn to defend.

Chapter 5 offers a realistic ethic of leadership with which to replace the leadership cult and its dangerous premise that the people on top got there via their virtue. Leaders need to know that their positions inevitably involve them in some measure of immorality. By keeping in mind that leadership is always morally ambiguous, leaders can replace dangerous false pride with moral caution that will help them do better than otherwise.

In Bush's business career, as chapter 4 shows, he at least once betrayed values he meant to uphold. Others have pointed accusing fingers at Bush's 1990 sale of stock in Harken Energy, but this book does far more. It analyzes documents showing that Bush may have acted criminally and certainly wrongly in that stock sale. As a board member with negative inside information, he had a moral obligation to share the fate of outside investors until they knew what he knew.

Yet just months earlier, as chapter 3 shows, Bush showed admirable moral leadership in blocking a Harken deal that would have unfairly injured small investors. Such good deeds can be a source of false pride. Exacerbated by the leadership cult, false pride can help blind leaders to wrongdoing, which may have been the case with Bush's inside selling.

Why Bush's business school education in leadership was not well suited to correct some of his youthful bad tendencies—especially arrogance and a careless neglect of the devil in the details—is the subject of chapter 2. His favoring of values-based leadership over hands-on management derives at least partly from the business school doctrine that leaders and managers have discrete personalities and functions. If leaders are taught that their jobs are essentially moral, they are less likely to soil their hands on mundane operations.

Chapter 1 analyzes the moral errors in the leadership cult. To try to use moral influence is to surrender unwittingly to immorality. Leaders who try to use morality run the risk of subordinating it to some ulterior purpose. If they slip into such unwitting hypocrisy, they are ripe for further corruption.

The conclusion of this book offers a more realistic approach to the moral challenges of leadership. Leaders cannot legitimately try to use moral influence. They should only try to earn moral influence, which requires using power as honestly as possible. That requires ethical understanding, situational knowledge, and professional competence.

All of us—followers as well as leaders—have a responsibility for moral leadership. The principle that in a democracy the people rule is only another way of saying that moral leadership is also the job of followers. The democratic idea that morality is as likely to be bottom-up as top-down is more realistic than the leadership cult's implicit faith that goodness descends from the executive suite.

In today's climate of morally erroneous ideas on leadership, every citizen has a great opportunity to become a genuinely moral leader. We should seize that opportunity by rejecting moral pretense in our leaders and in ourselves. By refusing to claim the mantle of moral leadership, we will have taken the first step toward earning it.

Chapter 1

The Leadership Cult and the MBA President

President Bush often uses values to lead. Yet polls have shown that a majority of Americans doubt his integrity.[1] That's not a coincidence. A leader who attempts to use values can easily subvert those values.

Think of the photo opportunity by which Bush will most likely be remembered. In April 2003 he flew in a fighter jet to the aircraft carrier Abraham Lincoln and made a dramatic tail-hook landing. After exchanging his flight suit for a business suit, he announced to cheering sailors and a worldwide television audience the end of major combat operations in Iraq. As the world knows, he had his facts wrong.

But he also had his ethics wrong. The problem was not that the flight was meant to win support for his 2004 reelection campaign. Leadership can involve dramatic gestures.

The ethical problem was that Bush's flight was only drama, only empty theatrics. The aircraft carrier was within easy reach of the presidential helicopter, making the fighter jet unnecessary. Bush's flight had the appearance but not the reality of martial valor.

Bush may not have understood his error in falsely trying to use valor to lead. In fact, he may have meant well. Nevertheless, the image he conveyed to a watching world was false.

Of course all leaders, like all the rest of us, lie some of the time. But the lies of today's leaders sometimes have a different cause than ordinary human weakness. Their lies also result from the widely prevalent idea of using values to lead.

For example, business leaders who try to make integrity a corporate value because they think honesty pays are in danger of corrupting themselves.

They can easily end up valuing manna more than morals. We should try to make money honestly. But we should not use honesty to make money.

If money becomes a motive for morality, profit may trump probity when the two values conflict. Honesty that is not its own reward easily becomes dishonesty in disguise. Leaders who use values for ulterior purposes may become, unaware, the agents of their own corruption.

Sometimes leadership becomes valued as an end in itself, making personal ambition its only motive. Although ambition is never absent in leaders, it is often offset by values shared with followers. But when vain ambition for leadership entirely eclipses the goals of followers, leadership is entirely corrupt.

That Bush values leadership to a morally dangerous degree is suggested by a 1999 conversation he had with a ghost writer working on his campaign autobiography. The writer was later taken off the project, possibly because the book was becoming too frank.[2] The future president said:

> One of the keys to being seen as a great leader is to be seen as a commander-in-chief. My father had all this political capital built up when he drove the Iraqis out of Kuwait and he wasted it. *If I have a chance to invade … , if I have that much capital, I'm not going to waste it. … I'm going to have a successful presidency.*[3]

National security is a national leader's first responsibility. A politician should use leadership to achieve national security. He should not use issues of national security to achieve leadership.

James Madison, one of the main authors of the U.S. Constitution, never heard of the leadership cult. But he understood the moral dangers of leadership and warned that a vain president might lead us into a mistaken war:

> It is in war, finally, that laurels are to be gathered, and it is the executive brow they are to encircle. The strongest passions, and most dangerous weaknesses of the human breast: ambition, avarice, vanity, the honorable or venial love of fame are all in conspiracy against the desire and duty of peace.[4]

Such moral danger in today's fashionable notions of moral leadership has been largely ignored. Check the leadership pulp at any mass market bookstore. The how-to manuals run on endlessly about the importance of values in leadership with scarcely a hint of the moral danger in using values to lead.

Recent books on leadership recommend many different values as the key to success. To be safe, therefore, a leader should probably value all of the following:

Integrity	Courage	Clarity
Credibility	Authenticity	Will
Trust	Responsibility	Conviction
Commitment	Transparency	Accountability
Joy	Daring	Character

If such a person could be found, he or she should be a candidate not just for leadership but for sanctification, provided only that humility were added to the list.

The idea that leaders are distinguished by their high values underlies the major leadership model of recent years—transformational leadership. Conventional wisdom distinguishes between transactional and transformational leaders. Transactional leaders are unimaginative types who use power to reward high performers and punish laggards. But transformational leaders either inspire followers to more faithfully uphold old values or inspire them to move toward new values. Either way, the followers are transformed.

This description of transformational leadership as based on values is probably right. But not all *descriptions* can be turned into *prescriptions*. Descriptions of good basketball players often include above-average height. But the prescription for improving one's game is not to try to be tall.

Basketball players improve their game by working on their skills and their knowledge of the game. Similarly, the way for leaders to improve their chance at morality is by developing professional competence, situational knowledge, and ethical understanding. Such skills and knowledge will help them manage *for* values.

To manage by values in the hope of becoming a moral leader is like trying to improve your basketball game by becoming taller. Not only will you not get taller, but you may weaken your game. In short, managing by values may make you a less moral leader.

Why is there so little understanding of the moral danger in trying to use values to lead? After all, religious tradition and folk wisdom have long cautioned against false pride and emperors without clothes. But some management gurus have ignored centuries of warning against the danger of self-righteousness.

One reason for the management gurus' error is that they aim to give corporate leaders what they need to succeed. But what if integrity is not what leaders always need to succeed? What if, at least sometimes, it is easier and more profitable to lead a company hypocritically than honestly?

There is an obvious but little discussed incentive for deceit in the leadership advice industry. Corporate executives pay good money for ideas that work well and look nice. If a deceitful idea works well, both seller and buyer may be tempted to box, wrap, and trim it in moral niceties that hide its mendacity from themselves as well as others. That is what has happened with the popular but mistaken idea of using values to manage.

I know too many leaders and leadership teachers to accuse them of deliberate hypocrisy as a group. Many of their teachings and techniques are not only useful but morally instructive. Many leadership gurus are fine people and a force for good, not just in business, but in democratic society at large. But in their ideas on the moral basis of leadership, some of them have gone astray.

Of course, many management gurus and business school professors are well aware that leadership imperils the character. Most of them will warn that power can corrupt. But too many fail to see that rather than reducing that risk, they increase it when they teach that morality and values can be used to lead.

With good will but unrealistic optimism, some leadership gurus have encouraged false confidence in human goodness. Leaders need true confidence, including confidence that they understand the moral imperfection of the world in general and human nature in particular. But false moral confidence slides easily into moral arrogance, which can be a leader's ethical undoing and, sometimes, practical undoing as well.

One way that the leadership cult inspires false moral confidence is by failing to teach leaders how difficult it can be to know what one values. When we proudly claim to have a value, we may only be paying lip service to it. For example, some parents who are seldom seen at their kids' baseball or soccer games proudly and mistakenly claim to have "family values." They probably do not even know that they value something else, maybe money or work, more highly than family.

Much of traditional religion teaches that the human heart can be so obscure that we cannot be certain that we know our own motives, let alone know them to be worthy. Much of modern psychology concurs as to the difficulty of self-knowledge. The truth is that it can be hard to discover what values we already hold, let alone "adopt" new values as some management gurus urge organizations to do.

The difficulty of knowing one's own values invalidates many narratives of leadership, especially some popular first-person chest thumpers from business leaders. This book avoids such subjective accounts. Instead, it relies on objective evidence from Bush's business career and from his presidency to show how a leader who tries to use values may end up subverting them.

The object of this book is not to condemn George Bush, but to learn from his mistakes. For all I know, George Bush is, at heart, as decent a person as many of us. In fact, I think that he probably is.

But that is faint praise. On decency, after all, our species has a sadly mixed record. The moral inadequacy of all human beings is what makes the self-righteousness encouraged by the leadership cult so dangerous.

Some of Bush's errors may well be due less to any flaws in his character than to his business education and business experience. Among previous presidents, only Herbert Hoover and, perhaps, Bush's father brought more corporate experience to the White House. And neither Hoover nor the elder Bush went to business school. As the first MBA president and as a veteran of many years of corporate life, Bush has been more exposed than any of his White House predecessors to the cult of moral leadership.

Bush has proclaimed his faith in his values and principles as his moral guides. This book argues that such an idea of the moral life is too limited. It is also too consistent with the leadership cult.

We can find additional moral resources to complement our values. By understanding the world's ethical complexity, we can better support our good values and improve our chances of successfully combating our bad ones. Through knowledge of the situations in which we must act, we improve our chances of seeing what's right. And professional competence improves our chance of successfully doing what's right.

Incompetence characterized Bush's worst presidential error, his decision to invade Iraq and his failure to plan for the aftermath of the invasion.[5] As it became evident that Bush had only a back-of-the-envelope strategy for pacifying Iraq, *Business Week* opined that we were entitled to expect better planning from an MBA president. That's partly true but partly false.

Yes, business students learn to plan. They plot scenarios, weigh strategies, and analyze Strengths, Weaknesses, Opportunities, and Threats (SWOT analysis). Everyone but the insurgents and the terrorists would have been better off if George Bush had put such skills to work figuring out the right policy in Iraq.

But business students also learn the conventional wisdom that leading is different from managing. The following quotation is from a textbook admirably critical of the conventional wisdom it summarizes:

Management is frequently associated with task focused responsibilities coordinated through hierarchical organisational structures. **Leadership** focuses on energising staff with a sense of direction and commitment through promotion of a collective sense of purpose engaging the "hearts and minds" of organisation members.

Leadership has become highly fashionable in recent times. This reflects increasing emphasis on inspiring people and encouraging their participation, over more dictatorial or bureaucratic approaches often associated with management.[6]

According to the leadership cult, leaders win followers through inspiration. Mundane managers, on the other hand, rely on power and position. Is it any wonder that a president like Bush, well tutored in corporate culture, seems to prefer the glamorous job of leading by values over the gritty job of hands-on management?

That Bush sees it as his job not to get his hands dirty in the details but to lead in the light of his values is supported by the story of his Oval Office rug, which he often relates to visitors:

He shared a story of one of the first decisions he was asked to make in the Oval Office. What style of rug would he want? He chuckled and explained to the questioner to ask Laura … as he didn't do rugs. He used that as a metaphor to explain how he manages the awesome responsibility he has. His role is to focus on the big decisions utilizing his core convictions that the United States is a force for good in the world. … He spoke very eloquently about good vs. evil and even brought the story back to the rug, which was designed with only this Presidential input … to let it reflect light so as to influence his decision making. Light as in good vs. darkness as in evil.[7]

The truth is that managerial power and moral leadership are not separate. Good management earns the moral influence by which leaders win followers. And in turn, moral leadership leavens managerial power.

But there can be no entirely satisfactory reconciliation between power and morality. Because corporate executives possess managerial power, they cannot be purely moral leaders, influencing followers solely by values. Corporate leaders are morally tainted by their power the moment they obtain it. That's not their fault, but the fault of the morally imperfect world in which we live.

Clips from Richard Attenborough's great film, *Gandhi*, are a staple of leadership training sessions. It is good for executives to consider the example of Gandhi who, armed only with holiness, took on the British Empire. But Gandhi makes suitable food for thought for CEOs only if they remember that their power makes them a good deal more like the British viceroy than the sainted leader of the Indian independence movement.

Only by remembering that they are morally tainted by their power can business leaders hope to achieve some measure of the moral caution they need. The goal of all executives should be to try to use their power only as effectively as is consistent with justice. Awareness of that goal's impossibility is, paradoxically, a condition of coming as close as possible to achieving it.

The leadership cult can adversely affect not only leaders' morality but also their practicality. The conventional wisdom that moral leadership and hands-on management are distinct activities can encourage leaders to pay too little attention to strategy and execution. Since leading is supposedly so much more courageous, creative, and effective—not to mention pleasing to the leader's vanity—why manage?

The temptation to ignore the hard work of managing in favor of the enjoyable job of leading is one of the causes of today's crisis of business ethics. At least some leaders caught in recent business scandals went wrong not just by corruption but by incompetence. Like George Bush with regard to Iraq, some CEOs have gone wrong by doing too much leading and not enough managing.

Ken Lay of Enron was a good example of the danger of trying to substitute moral leadership for managerial competence. Instead of managing Enron, he preferred to lead by preaching on the company's values, such as "integrity" and "respect," which were emblazoned on banners, elevators, and even parking garages at the company's Houston headquarters. Lay would have done better to have spent his time improving his competence in accounting. Even after Enron's demise he still did not comprehend the deals by which his subordinates had looted the company.[8]

And Lay sometimes genuinely held himself to high standards of behavior. In Enron's last desperate days, he negotiated a merger with Dynegy that seemed to have saved Enron and, in the process, netted him $61 million. But when subordinates protested, he agreed to turn down the $61 million in order to support employee morale.[9]

Lay's declining of $61 million became moot when the Dynegy merger fell through and, with it, Enron's last chance to avoid collapse. But the incident shows that Lay really did try to lead by values.

Lay's notion that leadership was mainly a matter of cheerleading may have helped induce the lies about the company's financial health for which he was ultimately convicted. His obituaries placed too much weight on his flawed character and too little on his bad ideas about leadership. A typical posthumous comment in the media was that while the Enron scandal led to reforms in business school curricula, "there are some things you can't … teach in business school. Sound business judgment is one of them."[10] But you can teach bad ideas that corrode character and encourage bad judgment.

More than a few CEOs now in jail or headed there have followed this flawed logic, even if they never put it into syllogistic form:

Leadership is a matter of exemplary values;
I am a leader;
Therefore, I must be a person of exemplary values.

If we begin by lying to ourselves about how good we are, we're on a slippery slope from the start. A useful, though not perfect, moral safeguard for leaders and the rest of us is to remember that most of us are people of middling decency. Keeping in mind that we are most likely as far removed from Gandhi's goodness as Hitler's evil can help fight off the self-righteousness promoted by the leadership cult.

Whether or not it is the leadership cult that has induced him to do so, George Bush has spoken more self-righteously than any president in living memory. So it is no surprise that he is now considered dishonest by a majority of citizens. Instead of assuring us that there is such a thing as moral clarity, he would have done better to have quoted Thomas Jefferson's warning that leaders even more than the rest of us are susceptible to self-deception: "Power believes it has a great soul and vast views, beyond the comprehension of the weak; and that it is doing God's service while it is violating all his laws."[11]

Bush's leadership style more than any particular act in his business career links him to Ken Lay, Bernie Ebbers, and their ilk. Bush's profit on the stock sale described in chapter 4 of this book was small potatoes compared to what Lay made at Enron and Ebbers at WorldCom. But Bush shares Lay's fondness for pontificating on values as well as Ebbers's predilection for opening business meetings with prayer.

Revelations of wrongdoing by self-proclaimed moral leaders have not alerted the business world to the moral danger of the leadership cult. CEOs' prevailing idea is that a few of their brethren failed as moral leaders. So rather than addressing the real issue—morally mistaken ideas on leadership—executives have relied on those same old bad ideas. Instead of recognizing the moral danger in trying to use values to lead, business leaders have renewed their emphasis on managing by values.

In the past few years I've heard a dozen CEOs do their post-Enron bit for ethics by preaching to business school students on the importance of values. These well-meaning but ethically callow corporate chiefs sound more than a little vain and sanctimonious. With their excessive confidence in their morality, they are too close for comfort to Ken Lay and Bernie Ebbers in their glory days.

There are plenty of articles by business school professors pondering the irony that some of the most criminal companies, such as Enron, were the ones who spoke most loudly about values. But the articles always conclude that leaders have to work all the harder on values issues. No one seems to get it that the problem is not that leaders are working too little on values. The problem is that some of them are working on values in an unwittingly corrupt way because of a bad idea in the leadership cult, the idea of using values to lead.

Most of the able managers and bright business school students I have met or taught are decent people with good instincts. Many of them have characters and common sense strong enough to survive their encounters with the leadership cult. They already know that morally pretentious leadership is as likely as managerial power to promote arrogance and blind the conscience.

But too many others find the leadership cult appealing. They need to be taught its moral dangers. Such understanding may help leaders deal better with the temptations of power. Indeed, such ethical understanding is their best defense against moral arrogance. Ethical understanding does not necessarily come cheap. Integrity may sometimes cost us business success rather than help us achieve it. Sometimes ethics requires us to do the unprofitable thing. Sometimes integrity is a cost, not a resource.

Too many business people think they can resolve the problem of business ethics with the reassuring assertion that honesty pays. That's wrong or, rather, a partial truth. Honesty only pays some of the time. Dishonesty pays some of the time, too.

The business leaders who preach that honesty always pays are, alas, in earnest. For like most of us they believe too uncritically in their own virtue. Their false moral confidence combined with their monetary success makes plausible to them the idea that riches result from righteousness.

The obvious moral danger in attributing one's success to one's sanctity makes it no less likely that leaders will do so. Moral delusion does not mount frontal attacks on the ego. False pride is a fifth column that burrows within, using furtive appeals to vanity to undermine common sense.

The defense of personal character is therefore the work not of a moment but of a lifetime, especially for leaders. CEOs and senior managers need constant reminding that top floor offices are not necessarily occupied by lofty souls. A position of leadership is more reason, not less, for concern about the state of one's morals.

Of course, upright leaders succeed a lot of the time. That's especially true of leaders who are not only moral but competent. Know-how often makes it possible to get results in the right way.

But the leadership cult wrongly suggests that moral leaders do their jobs by inspiring others. It's really the other way round. Moral leaders inspire others by doing their jobs.

There is a much closer link than is usually understood between charisma and competence. The same goes for situational knowledge and ethical understanding. So equipped, a leader has a fair shot at success even if he or she is honest! By contrast, a leader who relies mainly on vision and values is far more likely to forfeit both character and charisma.

Unfortunately, we are in danger of being led more and more by vision and values. For the cult of moral leadership is widely shared. In the last quarter century, corporate culture has increasingly supplanted our democratic values.

The leadership cult's challenge to democratic values has caught most citizens unawares because management gurus clothe their ideas in egalitarian language such as employee participation and bottom-up power. It is therefore easy to miss the undemocratic nature of the gurus' emphasis on top-down morality. Democracy depends on the recognition that morality is as likely to flow from the bottom up as the top down.

Without privileged access to Bush's inner life, it is impossible to know for certain the personal origins and meaning of his unusually moralistic rhetoric. But his moralizing is consistent with the leadership cult and its implicit condescension to followers. It is no wonder that many Americans now belittle him in return.

When I began thinking about this book, Bush's approval ratings were in the stratosphere, and I feared that I would not get a hearing for my idea that his presidency is a disaster illustrating the danger of using values to lead. Now that his approval ratings are at all-time lows, the danger is reversed. It may be hard to get a hearing for the possibility that Bush's moral mistakes are not entirely his fault, hard to get a hearing for the possibility that he may be not only a guilty proponent but also a guileless victim of mistaken ideas about leadership.

This book relieves Bush's character of at least a bit of responsibility for his mistakes. Some of the responsibility falls on the popular idea of using values to lead. Some of course prefer to demonize Bush. But a book about the danger of unwitting moral arrogance should at least attempt to avoid self-righteous recrimination of others' errors, even errors as catastrophic as Bush's.

Both Democrats and Republicans may therefore dislike this book. My idea that Bush has some good values may offend his enemies. But that Bush has some good values is the best explanation I can find for the moral leadership—described in chapter 3—that he provided to Harken Energy.

Conversely, pro-Bush readers, few though they probably will be, may dislike my charge that he has made many moral errors. But as stated above, I admit that George Bush possesses some good values. The point of this book, after all, is that it often takes more than good values to do the right thing. It often takes ethical understanding, situational knowledge, and professional competence.

The leadership cult is even more dangerous in the political than in the corporate arena. It violates an underlying principle of the Constitution of the United States—a leader who is a moral exemplar one moment may be a moral menace the next. The temptations of power can seduce a leader today just as easily as, in scripture, Bathsheba did King David. That is why democracies distrust leaders and fence them in with checks and balances.

The leadership cult, in short, is a modern version of the moral vanity that has always tempted powerful people. Since the leadership cult in its modern form originated in the business world, it should be fought there as well as in the political arena. Business executives, no less than politicians, are subject to its moral dangers.

By rejecting three mistaken ideas, leaders can help guard themselves against the fate of possessing some good values but nevertheless being morally misled by the leadership cult. First, reject the fallacious idea that good values are a sufficient guide for moral decisions in favor of a focus on ethical understanding, professional competence, and situational knowledge. Second, reject the undemocratic notion that a position of leadership marks a person as morally superior in favor of the idea that leadership is a morally dangerous job. Third, reject the idea of managing *by* values in favor of managing *for* values.

If you are a leader you may find this program difficult, for it asks you to give up ideas that appeal to your vanity. Who would not like to believe, as today's cult of leadership encourages you to believe, that you are a moral exemplar? But it is only by resisting such vanity that leaders can avoid becoming emperors without clothes.

Recently, a manager in a highly respected company kindly wrote to me to praise my last book—*False Prophets: The Gurus Who Created Modern Management and Why Their Ideas Are Bad for Business Today* (2003). He thought, however, that my book's appeal to CEOs to abandon their moral pretense was wasted breath. He could "not begin to imagine a willingness among America's senior executives to abandon their cherished, self-ascribed (and rigorously reinforced by subordinates) moral authority."

I urge business leaders to prove him wrong. Earn your employees' respect by showing that you are not fools! Reject the vain pretensions of moral leadership so common in the corporate world today! No really self-respecting leader wants phony "moral authority" over cynical subordinates.

But in addition to the temptation of vanity there is another reason that corporate leaders may find it difficult to give up moral pretense. The false ideas on moral leadership so prevalent in today's corporate world can get bottom-line results. Hypocrisy can make for profitable management!

Nothing better proves that business is not exempt from the ambiguities of our morally imperfect world than the fact that it is sometimes easier and more profitable to lead a company hypocritically than honestly. If phony values and an ersatz culture succeed in deceiving followers, they can make life easier for leaders. Leaders who give up the moral pretense in the leadership cult may be rewarded only with a harder job and a greater need for competence and knowledge.

Yet business leaders who resist the leadership cult have another reward in addition to integrity. As corporate culture becomes ever more closely related to our political culture, leaders who fight off morally pretentious notions of leadership help to preserve democratic values. Such leaders are friends of free and open societies.

Democracy, we are told, is on the march. But so are the global economy and the ever expanding opportunities and temptations for false pride afforded by corporate life. The ethical challenge facing the business world is not just to prevent financial corruption and future Enrons. Business leaders and all the rest of us should resist the cult of moral leadership and its threat to democracy.

Chapter 2

The Education of a President

In the fall of 1973 when George Bush started his MBA classes at the Harvard Business School (HBS), he may have been surprised to find teaching on leadership that he liked. In some of his Harvard classes the privileged young Bush would learn ideas implying that a top-of-the-heap position reflects moral superiority to people in the middle and bottom of the pile. It was probably a refreshing contrast to his undergraduate experience at Yale where he had encountered and resented moral challenges to the American establishment and, by extension, his elite family.

Yale had passed through a cultural revolution during Bush's undergraduate years. When he matriculated in 1964, old Eli was a school for preppy WASPs, alcohol was the drug of choice, and American troops were "advisors" in Vietnam. When he graduated in 1968, the university was a diverse, hirsute, marijuana-smoking meritocracy where protestors against the war in Vietnam scorned the school song's vow of service "for God, for Country, and for Yale."

According to Bush's bitter recollection, Yale's radical chaplain insulted him in the autumn of his freshman year. That November his father had lost a U.S. Senate election in Texas. The chaplain, who had known the elder Bush as a fellow Yale student in the 1940s, offended the son, understandably, by telling him to his face that his father was beaten by a "better man."[1]

Family loyalty is usually an admirable virtue. But in Bush it seems to have precluded any sympathy for the Yale radicals and their guilty angst over their upper crust privileges. Fixing on the anti-war movement's moral weak spot, he found in the Yale leftists an "arrogance I hope I never have."[2] He evidently did not see the danger that refusal to question his top-tier privileges might point him in the same direction.

No scholar and certainly no grade-grubbing, upwardly mobile striver, Bush took little interest in his Yale courses. In prep school he had encountered an inspiring history teacher, which may explain his majoring in history at Yale. But there is no indication of anything other than perfunctory academic performance in his Yale career.

Instead of book learning, he focused on beer-swilling, frat-boy antics that had an underlying seriousness of purpose. Student social life sorted out the leaders and the lemmings. With his wide circle of friends and followers, Bush learned that he possessed leadership qualities even as prestigious schools like Yale began to challenge the headship pretensions of the WASP elite.

Since World War II, young men aspiring to political leadership had gone from college to the military. On graduating in 1968, while less-traditional Yalies burned their draft cards, Bush enlisted in the Texas Air National Guard. Family friends may have pulled strings to get him into a "champagne unit" filled with politicians' sons.[3]

A blur of questions surround Bush's service in the Guard. Did he join to escape Vietnam? He later told the *Dallas Morning News* that he was "not prepared to shoot my eardrum out with a shotgun in order to get a deferment." His enlistment record shows that he checked a box requesting *not* to be assigned overseas.

Yet he also later said that once he was in the Guard, he volunteered for a program that could have sent him to Vietnam. Perhaps he hoped to cover himself with glory as his father had done as a pilot in World War II. The wish to emulate his father as a combat pilot may have been what drove him to join the Guard in the first place. It was easier to qualify for flight training in the Guard than in the regular Air Force.

There is no contradiction between wanting to keep out of a bad fight and regretting the absence of a good one. Admiring the war record and political ambition of his father, young Bush may have felt a family duty to put on a uniform even if he believed the war was a waste. Such ambivalence about Vietnam was not uncommon among children of World War II vets.

Although he enjoyed his year of full-time flight training, Bush seems to have had little enthusiasm for his subsequent duties. Maybe the political work arranged by his father distracted him. In any case, his National Guard record was mixed at best.

In 1972 the Guard stripped Bush of his pilot's status for "failure to accomplish" a required physical examination. Did he fail the physical or fail to take it? Presumably there would be no shame in the former. But since Bush has refused to clear up the mystery, he may have failed to take it.

Why would he have skipped a physical exam? Bush's enemies have suggested that he feared it would reveal drug use.[4] But he may have just carelessly neglected to take it since he showed little interest in his Guard responsibilities that year.

Equally murky is the question of whether Bush put in his time. *U.S. News & World Report* examined the records and concluded that he did not. Required to attend 48 training drills a year, he showed up for only 36 in 1972. That same year he missed five months of training; and then, in his last year, 1973, he attended just nine drills.[5]

On the other hand, Albert Lloyd, a retired personnel official with the Texas Guard says Bush met his commitment. According to Lloyd, the Guard did not use calendar years but, rather, 12-month periods following the enlistment date. That makes Bush's service more creditable. Although Lloyd was paid for his opinion by Republican partisans, his insistence on beginning each year of service on the anniversary of Bush's enlistment makes sense. Otherwise, a December enlistee would be a shirker from the start.[6]

Still, there's the problem that Bush's superior officers in 1972 and 1973 report that he did not show up for duty. In September 1972 he applied for and was given a transfer from Houston to a unit in Montgomery, Alabama, where his father had arranged for him to work on a Republican senatorial campaign. Both the commanding officer and the personnel officer of the Alabama unit have no recollection of Bush.[7] After the November 1972 election, he returned to Houston and should have resumed duties there. But his Houston superior, in his annual review on May 1, 1973, stated that "Lt. Bush has not been observed at this unit during the period of report."[8]

Yet paper records suggest that Bush may have done some training in both Alabama and Houston during the period in question. He had dental work done at the former base, and he got paid for some service at the latter. The mystery may never be cleared up.

It is difficult to make this mixed evidence on Bush's military service reflect well on him. Maybe he put in his time but in ways so unimportant as to draw no attention from his superiors, especially after he was stripped of his wings. A grounded pilot who showed up for duty just to get marked present rather than to fly might have gotten little attention.

Whether that's what happened or not, the deeper truth is clear. If Bush had done his best, there would be no question that he met minimum standards of service. He seems to have been anxious to move on and to have given little attention to his Guard obligation.

Weak as Bush's record looks on the surface, it is important to remember that, as opposed to the Iraq War, the National Guard counted for little in the Vietnam era. If he had a careless attitude toward the Guard, he was scarcely unique at the time. What distinguished him was that, as a Bush, he faced larger temptations than other weekend warriors.

Bush's political enemies are over the top in saying that he failed his country. His country, fighting a limited and misbegotten war, didn't need him. If it had, a young man so eager for distinction as Bush would have gladly put himself in harm's way.

But if Bush means it when he says he is proud of his service, he would seem to be mistaken. His record seems more worthy of embarrassment. It suggests a spoiled youth who missed a needed lesson in how unforgiving reality can be, even to a Bush.

While losing interest in his duties as a weekend warrior, he was also losing interest in his weekday job as a corporate trainee. Through family connections he had found an entry-level job at a processor of agricultural and ranch products. It's hard to imagine George Bush happily riding a desk while making a career out of managing cattle feedlots and overseeing chicken slaughtering plants. Not surprisingly, he soon left the company for the opportunity that also marked the deterioration of his Guard performance, the chance to work in a Republican senatorial campaign in Alabama.

In those years his father yearned for the Senate and the White House. No wonder that the younger Bush—reverent and probably also rivalrous of his father—seems to have suffered from outsized political ambition. Friends and family dissuaded him from trying for a seat in the Texas State legislature by pointing out that he had no record on which to run.

A legal education was the traditional preparation for a political career. In 1972 Bush applied to the University of Texas Law School. Back came the rejection that his undergraduate record deserved.

Bush's failure to get into law school was in a way unfortunate for us as well as for him. Among the benefits of a legal education is an understanding of constitutional law. Knowledge of the founding fathers' distrust of leaders—expressed in constitutional limitations on the executive branch—might have alerted Bush to the moral dangers in the leadership cult.

At this point in his life, Bush had demonstrated some very good qualities. Energetic and lively, he was and would remain a strongly knit personality, possessing both some of the personal charm and some of the toughness that can make a leader. With the security that came from his fortunate upbringing and high social status, Bush had the personal solidity that can be the basis of great achievement.

But his flaws were not small. Not only was he undisciplined and irresponsible, he seemed not to have learned that privilege carries the risk of arrogance and restricted vision. There is no evidence to suggest that he searched out experiences that would have challenged and broadened his view of the world.

Denied admission to law school and its entrée to politics, Bush opted for his family's other occupational tradition. He would try to make big money. The Harvard Business School accepted him for the fall of 1973, despite his middling undergraduate record.

Bush may have hoped to find HBS students focused on marketing and finance, not politics. After his undergraduate encounter with Yale radicalism, an apolitical postgraduate education would likely have been to his taste. But even the Harvard Business School was tinged by the antiestablishment mood of the 1970s.

As the Vietnam War wound down, the Watergate scandal heated up. HBS Republicans called for President Nixon's resignation. Bush, whose father loyally served Nixon as chairman of the National Republican Committee, kept his distance from GOP activists at Harvard.

He had still less affinity for business students trying for a bit of radical cachet with long hair and beards. Many participated in a grape boycott to support migrant workers. Feminists staged a "pee-in" to protest a paucity of women's restrooms at the formerly all-male school.

Sartorially defying the liberals, Bush proudly sported a leather flight jacket signaling that he had jockeyed jets in the military. In class, he sat in the back row, chewed gum, and guzzled coffee. Finished with the java, he popped in a chaw of tobacco and spat the juice into his empty cup.

Not surprisingly, his classmates gave him a divided reception. His energy and fun attracted some of his fellow students. His cowboy-flyboy act alienated others.

One of his professors reports that Bush treated with contempt a required course in business and society. Seeing the course as a challenge to his conservative politics, Bush defended himself through ideological trench digging. Telling the professor that the New Deal was socialism, he could not articulate his reasons when challenged.[9]

Bush's contempt for his Harvard course in business and society was not necessarily all bad. Business school courses in business ethics, social responsibility, and the like can prompt self-righteous posturing by either the professor or students. Bush may have been put off by class-room moral arrogance.

But if indeed Bush found arrogance in some Harvard classes, he seems to have answered it in kind. Defiance is not unusual in a young person seeing more danger in a new ambiance than is really there. But such posturing can help confirm the bad habit of assuming superiority to others.

Yet in practical skills, Bush profited greatly from his HBS education. Business schools' emphasis on soft-touch human relations is good preparation not just for commerce but for politics. The old breed of curmudgeon bosses who step in it the minute they set foot in political pastures is giving way to a new line of MBA politicians who pride themselves on their human touch.

New York has an MBA mayor. Massachusetts and New Hampshire have recently had MBA governors, the former of whom, Mitt Romney, is running for the 2008 Republican presidential nomination.[10] With business schools churning out more than 100,000 advanced degrees per year, there will inevitably be more political leaders with MBAs.

Although business schools are increasingly influential not only in business but also in politics, the general public knows little about them. There is a widely prevailing misconception of business schools as a place where case-cracking grinds focus only on perfecting their analytical and quantitative skills. While I was writing this book, acquaintances would ask what it was about, and I tried a shorthand answer: "George Bush as the first MBA president." More often than not, the inquirer would nod sagely, confident that he or she understood the spirit of the MBA—a single-minded focus on the bottom line.

That's wrong. Of course, business students learn to calculate margins, break even points, and return on investment. But they learn a lot more than financial number crunching. They learn theories of organization and leadership that amount to an applied moral and social philosophy, some of which has undemocratic implications.

The popular business school theory of leadership by top-down moral influence would have perfectly fit Bush's desire to defend himself and his family against democratic challenges to the political and social establishment in the 1960s and 1970s. How could he not be drawn to a theory of leadership implying that the possession of power proves one morally worthy of it? Organizational Behavior (OB) was Bush's favorite Harvard course.

OB, the study of how people interact in organizations, is the political science of corporate life. Bush, with his family background in politics and his natural leadership qualities, could only have been stirred by the people-handling focus of OB. Participating enthusiastically in class discussion, he manifested intellectual excitement uncharacteristic of much of his educational career. A classmate remembered him as "pretty concerned about how organizations worked and how people worked in those organizations."[11]

OB focuses on the question of how to rally employees to get the best or the most work done in a cost-efficient way. The answer inevitably touches on universal moral issues such as power, justice, and the relation of the individual to society. Bush's OB course was probably the closest he ever came to formal study of moral philosophy.

Although the HBS archives contain no syllabi for Bush's time there, it is certain that he learned several big ideas. Employees, according to traditional OB orthodoxy, have bottom-up power. Leaders, therefore, have to rely not on authority but on moral influence. And such moral leaders are cut from a different cloth than spiritless managers.

Purportedly empirical evidence for two of these discoveries— bottom-up power and top-down moral leadership—came from the famous 1920s Hawthorne experiment. Conducted at a telephone assembly plant of that name near Chicago, the Hawthorne experiment was mistakenly thought to have shown that power had little to do with successful industrial leadership. That mistaken interpretation, which gave the Hawthorne experiment its still significant influence, was the work of professors at the Harvard Business School.[12]

During Bush's second year at Harvard, the business school mounted an exhibit commemorating the 50th anniversary of the Hawthorne experiment. And the student newspaper, the *Harbus*, proudly noted that human relations research began at Harvard.[13] Whether or not Bush took any notice of such extramural celebrations of the Hawthorne experiment, he would have imbibed its intellectual legacy in his OB class.

The Hawthorne experiment is remembered mainly for the "Hawthorne effect." Employees, according to HBS professors, raised their output for no other reason than that they enjoyed the interest they received as subjects of the experiment. Much of modern management's emphasis on sympathetic understanding and recognition of employees is a sensible attempt to generalize the Hawthorne effect into a people-handling technique. The tradition of organizational behavior built on the Hawthorne experiment no doubt does a lot of good by softening managers' unnecessary harshness.

But subsequent scholars have shown that the HBS professors misinterpreted the Hawthorne experiment. The Harvard professors theorized that the workers enjoyed the extra supervisory attention that resulted from the experiment. But in fact, Hawthorne workers disliked the intense observation to which the experiment subjected them and saw it as an invasion of their privacy.[14]

The Hawthorne workers did not raise their output because of more sympathetic management. Rather, they understood that the experimental protocol guaranteed that higher output would not lead management, in the time-honored fashion, to cut the rate they were paid per piece. High pay, not high morale, raised output at Hawthorne.

The spurious interpretation of the Hawthorne experiment was mostly the work of a charlatan professor named Elton Mayo who taught at HBS from the late 1920s to the late 1940s. A medical school dropout, Mayo pretended to be a doctor with strong research and scientific credentials. More than any other guru he created the style of modern corporate management with its underestimation of top-down power and its overestimation of top-down moral influence.

Flawed humanity is a sucker for the promise of easy money and effortless self-esteem. Mayo accordingly offered employers a cost-free method for raising productivity while promoting their belief that they were acting benevolently toward the lesser souls beneath them. By loosening managerial controls and encouraging workplace community, employers, in the too honest words of Mayo's disciples, could give "satisfaction" to employees and "profit" to themselves.[15]

The possibility of substituting employee satisfaction for higher pay as a means of motivation gave Mayo's ideas allure in the corporate world. As a complementary enticement, he provided a defense against any charge that managerial power contradicts democratic political values. According to Mayo, the secret of effective management is workplace freedom which allows employees to form organic communities and to work with a will.

Out of the tradition of Mayo and the Harvard Business School came the emphasis on bottom-up power, teamwork, and soft-touch human relations that have often proved more effective than the preceding tradition of supervisory harshness. But Mayo covered up the importance of top-down power by teaching that tangible rewards and punishments are irrelevant to employee élan. Ever since Mayo, management seers have often failed sufficiently to discriminate between two kinds of power—workers' bottom-up power to do the job and the boss's top-down power to reward or discipline the worker.

Confused overstatements of employees' bottom-up power then became an implicit argument for the idea that morality is top-down. For if employees have power, executives evidently do not. Therefore, corporate executives do not boss; they lead through moral influence.

The most influential early 20th-century proponent of the idea of moral leadership in business was a brilliant AT&T executive named Chester Barnard. Lecturing frequently at the Harvard Business School in the 1930s, Barnard built on Mayo's idea of bottom-up power. Since subordinates have power, Barnard reasoned that executives' responsibilities always exceed their authority.

Executives' lack of adequate authority is the paradoxical condition of their successful leadership, at least according to Barnard. By bravely shouldering the existential burden of responsibility without authority, a leader sets an example of moral courage. Followers, inspired by the leader's example, find the spirit to get the job done.

As with Mayo's ideas, Barnard's thoughts on leading by moral influence are propagated in organizational behavior courses like the one that briefly woke young George Bush from his academic slumbers. But Barnard's influence is not just academic. There is scarcely a management guru who does not treat the subject of leadership, in one way or another, as a matter of moral influence. And if the idea of leaders' moral superiority is not explicitly stated, it is all too often unwittingly implied in the ceaseless flood of management fads.

Part of the reason that some of Barnard's and Mayo's ideas still hold sway is that for all their exaggeration and even prevarication, their ideas contain an important core of truth. Employees often do have a lot of bottom-up power over their jobs, making their spirited participation vital to organizational success. And successful leadership often does involve top-down moral influence.

But Mayo and Barnard created moral dangers for aspiring moral leaders. By understating executives' top-down power, they minimized the need to be on guard against power's tendency to corrupt. They failed to warn that corporate bosses have their best shot at moral leadership less by using moral influence than by earning it. And the way to earn moral influence is to use managerial power not only as honestly but as competently as possible.

That it is right for a leader to earn moral influence but dangerous to use it is no easy sell since business executives need all the tools they can get. Told by gurus that moral influence is the secret of success, executives naturally want to put it to work. The trouble is that to try to use moral influence can be the first step toward corruption.

An executive who tries to put integrity to the service of profit may often succeed. Even if the leader forgets the value of honesty while using it, followers will not necessarily see their leader's corruption. But though such executives may retain their influence, they do so not as moral, but as immoral leaders.

A better device for the insidious corruption of executives could scarcely be imagined than the leadership cult. If a morally pretentious leader succeeds, he or she will attribute success to moral influence. From there it is only a short step for the leader to conclude that he or she is, indeed, a morally superior person when, in fact, he or she is exercising false pride.

These exaggerated and morally dangerous ideas—bottom-up power and top-down morality—were the intellectual basis for the organizational behavior course in which George Bush learned leadership at the Harvard Business School. In the midst of democratic challenges to established power in the late 1960s and early 1970s, it would be surprising if Bush did not find congenial the implicit HBS claim that morality supports social hierarchy. One imagines him in class eagerly absorbing ideas so well suited for justifying the privileges he enjoyed and which were being challenged almost everywhere else.

Bush may also have learned in his OB class the idea that leaders are leaders, managers are managers, and never the twain shall meet. By the 1970s, when he arrived at Harvard, OB had moved from observation of workers to psychoanalysis of leaders. One of the Harvard Business School's most prominent OB professors during Bush's time there was a psychoanalyst named Abraham Zaleznik.

Zaleznik's still widely influential *Harvard Business Review* article, "Managers and Leaders: Are They Different?" was not published until 1977, two years after Bush got his MBA. But the article reflected an idea that had long been developing at Harvard and has since grown commonplace in business schools and in the corporate world. Bush was probably exposed at Harvard or soon after, in his business career, to the idea that "managers and leaders are very different kinds of people."[16]

Although Zaleznik evenhandedly declared that we need both managers and leaders, moral superiority clearly lay with the latter. "It takes neither genius nor heroism to be a manager," Zaleznik declared, for such a "once born" personality, content with the status quo, accepts the organization as it is. But leaders—"great" and "twice born" souls—are "worthy of the drama of power and politics." By shaping followers' moods, expectations, and objectives, business leaders transform "the way people think about what is desirable, possible, and necessary."[17]

Ideas like Zaleznik's would surely have appealed to young George Bush. Leaders, according to Zaleznik, are often late bloomers because "people with great talents are often indifferent students." Struggling toward a second birth, these turbulent souls suffer from "self-absorption and the inability to pay attention to the ordinary tasks at hand."[18]

Indeed, history shows that some great leaders in their youth have seemed just as unpromising as Zaleznik said. But when those great leaders of the past slacked off in youth, they were surrounded by multitudes just like them who never amounted to anything. Applying the lessons of history to the present, it is clear that while some of today's leaders may be former slackers, most of today's slackers are not future leaders.

There is therefore a moral risk in exposing business students or anyone else to ideas like Zaleznik's. It's not that such ideas should not be taught, but they should be taught in a way that does not make mediocrity a virtue. Otherwise, if a lucky slacker makes it into a position of power, he or she may suppose that continued success depends not on the hard work of competent management but only on the seemingly easy job of moral leadership.

Zaleznik did better in this respect than many subsequent gurus by calling attention to the importance of "performance and integrity," which he saw as "antidotes to the power disease called *hubris*."[19] But he did not say exactly how a leader elicits performance and maintains integrity. Ever since, leadership gurus have given too little attention to the importance of competent and honest use of managerial power in achieving moral leadership.

Zaleznik saw little point in trying to make born leaders into managers or vice versa. "It is easy enough," he said, to call "for people who can be both" managers and leaders. But Zaleznik thought such appeals futile. Managers and leaders "differ in motivation, in personal history, and in how they think and act."[20]

This blanket assertion that managers and leaders are necessarily two different kinds of people is surely mistaken. Since Zaleznik offered no evidence for his assertion, it is fair to counter with common sense and personal experience. Is it really impossible that a few of those able to spot the devil is in the details may also be able to see the big picture? The best leaders for whom I have worked were just such people.

An organization wanting to develop people for its top positions should aim to find those who have not only the vision to soar but also the acuity to see what's happening on the ground. Unfortunately, corporate culture of the past thirty years has put the emphasis on leaders as opposed to leader-managers.

The cult of leadership as it has developed in business and increasingly the rest of society has tended to focus on the leader's supposed qualities of personality and spirit. Emphasis on charisma and character, or vision and values, tends to exclude mundane managerial ability. Now and then a researcher delightedly discovers and reports that managers and leaders are more alike than is usually thought. But the overall tendency is to see leadership as different from and superior to management.

The firmness of the boundary between leaders and managers is softened by the need of gurus and business school professors for a teachable message. Not many managers in search of executive education will pay good money for a course telling them that, if they are goats, they can never be sheep. So gurus and professors teach managers how to use values and moral influence to lead.

Overemphasis on moral influence is the primary ethical failing in today's cult of moral leadership. Under the influence of these ideas, vain executives can easily mistake conceit and delusion for the vision and values supposedly characteristic of leaders. Living in such dream castles, executives can remain undaunted by objective failure of performance while incompetently relying on values to lead.

Wise executives do not take the leadership cult seriously. They understand that honest and competent management is a basis of leadership, not its antithesis. But tyrants and tyros, crooks and fools—the Bernie Ebbers and Ken Lays—easily succumb to the vanity of believing themselves large souls who lead mainly by values and vision.

What moral effect might the teaching of such dangerous, exaggerated, and false notions—top-down morality, bottom-up power, and the unbridgeable chasm separating leaders from managers—have on a young man of privilege? What if he were blessed with some personal attractiveness and natural leadership ability? What if he were also confident but careless, resentful of moral arrogance in others but indulgent of it in himself, possessed of some personal integrity but uneducated in ethics?

It would not be surprising if such a man with such an education, seeing obvious wrongdoing by his associates, led them to do better, especially if the integrity in question came at little cost to him personally. But when he did the right thing he would be poorly prepared to guard against—and indeed, might be more than normally susceptible to—false pride in his own virtue. So in a subsequent case involving profit not for others but for him, he might self-righteously believe he could rely on his supposedly good values for moral guidance and thereby fall into wrongdoing of his own.

Chapter 3

Moral Leadership at Harken Energy

With his MBA in hand, 28-year-old George Bush gladly departed Harvard and what he called its "heaviness," so burdensome to the entrepreneurial personality he considered himself to be. He wanted open spaces, welcoming to "do-ers." Oil prices were surging during the mid-1970s energy crisis, so he headed back to booming Texas.

By hanging around the Midland, Texas, courthouse, Bush learned the oil business. Researching deeds and mineral rights, he advised "land men" what lots were worth a speculative bid. His name opened the doors of local rainmakers. His brash charm kept the portals ajar.

A titular resident of the Lone Star state since the age of four, Bush was nevertheless not all Texan. His New England pedigree, prep school education, and Ivy League degrees, not to mention his tasseled loafers, marked him as an interloper. But he had long since developed personal habits—hard swearing and hard drinking—that overcame xenophobic suspicions in the oil crowd.

The rest of West Texas was tougher to convince. Eventually, he looked natural enough in a Stetson and boots to win the governorship. But he lost a premature 1978 bid for a seat in Congress after his Democratic opponent tarred him as a carpetbagger.

The next year, 1979, he started his own oil company and named it "Arbusto," Spanish for Bush. An uncle on Wall Street helped him raise capital, often from the same people who wrote checks for his father's political campaigns. The price of crude oil more than doubled during 1979, and investors were eager to get in the game.

Bush achieved, at best, a mixed record as an oilman. He claimed to have purchased valuable reserves but brought in no gushers. As oil prices declined in the early 1980s, Arbusto began to lose money. By changing Arbusto's name to Bush Exploration, he foiled the local wits who called him "Are-busted." But he did not stem the losses. Bush's investors were soon out millions, their pain mitigated by generous tax write-offs that Congress in those days provided for oil industry losses.

Whether through luck, connections, or skill—maybe a bit of all three—Bush made a deal that kept his oil career alive. In early 1984 an investment firm called Spectrum 7 merged with Bush Exploration and put him at the head of the new company, also called Spectrum 7. Bush got a $75,000 salary and a million shares of stock.[1]

But the failure of oil prices to rise laid the new firm low. In 1986 Bush sold Spectrum 7 to Harken Energy, a larger Texas oil company. In this new deal, Bush negotiated for himself a seat on the Harken Board of Directors, common stock worth more than $300,000, and options on more shares.

Harken also promised Bush consulting work that would pay between $50,000 and $120,000 a year, a substantial income at the time.[2] The likelihood is that it was not Bush's consulting expertise but his name that Harken wanted. The company would find it useful to have as a director the son of the Vice President of the United States.

Bush's consulting income allowed him to keep his base in Texas while focusing on Washington. He devoted 1988 to his father's presidential campaign. After the elder Bush's 1989 inauguration, the younger George Bush had the free time to play an unofficial role in the new administration.

His main activity back in Texas seems to have been attendance at meetings of the Harken board, on which he now served. Harken had grown adept at fast financial footwork and needed Bush's good values. The company's down-home founder lamented the "promotion, manipulation and inside deal making" that had turned Harken into a "fast-numbers game."[3]

Hard times in the oil patch made it tempting to fiddle with the books. With petroleum prices down, there was little profit in drilling wells. Some at Harken saw an easier road to riches in a combination of quick deals and creative accounting.

In 1989 Harken sold a string of Hawaiian gas stations called "Aloha." The buyer was Intercontinental Mining and Resources (IMR), a shell company of Harken insiders. In theory, the insiders "paid" Harken $12 million for Aloha. In reality, they forked over just $1 million and promised to pay the additional $11 million over seven years, out of Aloha revenues. Even though Harken only had the first million dollars in hand from the Aloha sale, it booked the entire $12 million as revenue for 1989, enabling it to show an immediate gain of $7.9 million on the deal.

Perhaps just as bad, Harken retained environmental liability for leaky underground gasoline tanks at Aloha. In other words, Harken insiders, wearing their IMR hat, took Aloha's assets but not its liabilities. That left Harken's common shareholders bearing the burden for yet to be determined environmental damage.

But the days when robber barons answered only to their own puny consciences were long gone. In 1991 the Securities and Exchange Commission (SEC) required Harken to restate its 1989 earnings. The $11 million Aloha note could not be counted as revenue till it was actually paid in cash.

Bush served on Harken's audit committee while the accounting shenanigans were going on. It is not clear whether the audit committee was lazy, careless, incompetent, dishonest, or deceived. Bush's later answer to critics that accounting practices are subject to differences of opinion is true but beside the point. Harken's disagreement was not with just anyone but with the SEC whose job is to protect investors against misleading accounting. And the SEC found misleading accounting at Bush's company.

Harken gave Bush another reason to squirm uncomfortably at the end of 1989 when the company got what could have been one of the great sweetheart deals of all time. The Kingdom of Bahrain gave Harken a contract to drill offshore in the Gulf of Bahrain. The site was next door to Saudi Arabia, home of the world's largest proven oil reserves.

It is an interesting question why the Bahrainis would have given such a choice opportunity to an oil company little known in America, let alone the Middle East. Harken had never drilled under water or outside the United States. In fact, it is not clear that Harken at this point did much drilling at all. Its 10Q filing for June 1990 shows that more than 98 percent of its revenue came from its pipelines and gas stations. The "Exploration and Production" part of the business seems to have been moribund.

The truth is that Harken was little more qualified to drill in the Gulf of Bahrain than your neighborhood pet shop. It subcontracted the work to German and Dutch companies. The only capability Harken brought to the Bahrain contract was the deal making at which the company had become all-too adept. Harken's real goal seems to have been to skim off all the money it could by acting as middleman between Bahrain and the subcontractors. In the end, however, the project yielded nothing. Harken's subcontractors drilled two dry holes in the Gulf of Bahrain.

What could possibly have made the Bahrainis choose to do business with a company so obviously unqualified as Harken? One account has it—unlikely as it seems—that the initial contact between Harken and the Bahrainis was a matter of good luck eagerly battened onto by Harken managers. The Bahrainis were searching for a company small enough to view the contract as a big deal and give it high priority. They consulted American advisors and investment bankers, one of whom had done business with Harken in the past.[4]

But even if chance contacts first led the Bahrainis to Harken, the question remains why they did not keep on searching? Why did they give their contract to an utterly unqualified company that conceived of its mission less as drilling for oil than making a killing as middleman? The answer surely had something to do with the Bahrainis' delight in the fact that the son of their dear friend, the President of the United States, was on Harken's board.

When the elder George Bush had been vice president in the 1980s, he had been point man for the Reagan administration in dealing with Bahrain. He seems to have won the Bahrainis' affection, demonstrations of which were not subtle. In 1986, for example, the Bahrainis gave President and Mrs. Reagan four dozen roses while Vice President Bush got a $15,000 Rolex. On Barbara Bush the Bahrainis lavished a $40,000, 18-karat, gold-and-diamond watch plus $30,000 worth of jewelry. The Bushes turned the loot over to the U.S. government, as they were required to do by law.[5]

In 1989 the Bahrainis were all the more eager to keep on friendly terms with the elder George Bush, who now resided in the White House. The tiny kingdom of Bahrain needed American help in guarding its oil reserves against avaricious and outsized neighbors like Iraq and Iran, a need soon to be demonstrated by the 1990 Iraqi invasion of Kuwait and the resulting Gulf War. The Bahrainis' past gifts to the Bushes showed how they thought affectionate ties were maintained. Obviously, the Bahrainis gave their drilling contract to Harken at least partly because they believed that the way to the heart of the President of the United States was through the lining of his son's pockets.

George W. Bush was sensitive to charges of misusing his name. In 1991, when a *Wall Street Journal* reporter asked if his being the president's son was behind Harken's getting the Bahrain contract, he snapped, "Ask the Bahrainis."[6] He later insisted that he had nothing to do with Harken's getting the Bahrain contract.[7]

Bush should scarcely have been surprised or resentful that others would think he had sold his name. He had accepted a well-paid Harken "consulting" job even though it is not clear that he had anything to offer management other than the influence of the Bush family name in places like Bahrain. If indeed Bush opposed the deal in board discussions, that does not change the likelihood that Harken got the Bahrain contract because he was on the company's board.

Yet Bush's service on the Harken board was, on at least one occasion, more than honorable. For a brief moment in his Harken career, Bush acted in a spirit of moral leadership that would be good for any company. Enron might well have avoided its collapse if someone on its board had behaved with as much integrity as, at one point, Bush did on Harken's. He stood up to some company insiders who wanted to raise cash for the Bahraini operations at the expense of small shareholders.

Harken was in a liquidity crisis all through the spring of 1990. Part of the problem was heavy debt from trading losses. Enron was one of its partners in some trades. Harken was sensibly exiting the trading business, but substantial damage had been done.

On the plus side, Harken had two valuable subsidiaries—a natural gas and pipeline company named Tejas Power and a chain of gas stations and convenience stores called E-Z Serve. Tejas Power generated a steady cash flow. So did E-Z Serve.

But despite its valuable pipelines and gas stations, Harken could not get a bank loan to resolve its liquidity crisis in the spring of 1990. That was not surprising since Harken was unable to meet its present obligations and was having to grant creditors new concessions and property liens in return for easier payment terms on existing loans. The Bahrain project might or might not deliver income to service more debt. Banks would want to see improvement in Harken's liquidity and long-term viability before making any new commitments.

The board briefly considered a new stock issue to resolve the liquidity crisis. But Smith Barney, Harken's financial consultant, advised that with oil prices down, the market had little appetite for new stock from energy companies. A public offering was unlikely to raise the cash the company needed.

Reorganization in bankruptcy court might have been a logical step. Bankruptcy, however, would have relieved the company not only of its

debts but also of its board and senior management. The Harken directors and managers seem, understandably, to have wanted to stay aboard
their leaky vessel.

By keeping themselves at the helm, the directors and managers could
participate to the fullest degree in the Bahrain deal. But neither a public
offering nor a bank loan was available to keep Harken afloat. Some
more creative method would have to be found in order, as the board
minutes put it, to "infuse" cash into the company.

Flush insiders or "major shareholders" as the Harken minutes refer
to them, seemed the best source of new cash for the company. But the
major shareholders understood Harken's risks as well as anyone. In
return for putting in more money, the major shareholders would need a
guaranteed return on their investment.

Someone at Harken—probably the major shareholders themselves—
came up with a plan. Harken would spin off its profitable pipelines (Tejas
Power) as well as its gas stations and convenience stores (E-Z Serve) as
independent companies. A "rights offering" giving Harken's present
stockholders a chance to buy shares in the two new companies at an
"attractive price" would raise desperately needed cash for Harken.[8]

The breakup of Harken would be a winning deal for shareholders
since the market would value the subsidiaries more highly once they
were on their own. Harken was identified with cyclical drilling and
therefore suffered low market valuation when oil prices were down, as
they were in 1990. But in fact, Harken was not so cyclical. It enjoyed
steady revenue and earnings from Tejas Power's pipelines and from E-Z
Serve's gas stations and convenience stores. With their reliable cash flow
and steady earnings, these spun-off companies should command a
higher price in the market, raising shareholder value.

Harken would get desperately needed cash from the spinoff of Tejas
Power and E-Z Serve. For the board maintained that Harken had provided assets and services to the new companies that required compensation in the form of cash payments to their corporate parent. In addition,
banks were willing to extend $20 million in new loans provided that the
major shareholders guaranteed that the rights offering would raise $40
million.[9]

And the current Harken directors and managers would get control of
a goodly amount of that cash. The Harken Executive Committee sol-
emnly averred that the present board and senior management "consti-
tuted an appropriate management group" for the new "exploration and

production subsidiary."[10] They would retain the Harken name and the Bahrain contract.

To guarantee the raising of $40 million in new capital from the rights offering, the major shareholders would commit themselves to "stand by," ready to exercise any purchase rights not exercised by Harken's small shareholders. That seemed a good proposition for the major shareholders since the shares were to be attractively priced and since Tejas Power and E-Z Serve, with their steadier businesses, would be less risky than Harken. In addition, the major shareholders would get a small percentage of the deal as a fee for their guarantee of its success in raising $40 million. These benefits to the major shareholders seemed above board and proportionate to the size of their investment which, after all, was going to save the company.

But then came a slipperier part of the deal. The major shareholders proposed to exchange their holdings of Harken preferred stock for common shares. On the face of it this made good business sense for all concerned since the preferred stock had a high, guaranteed dividend. By spinning off its pipelines and gas stations, Harken would also be shedding most of its steady revenue and could therefore not support the guaranteed dividend while waiting to strike it rich in Bahrain.

But what would be a fair rate of exchange for the preferred stock? The major shareholders wanted an "inducement." An exchange ratio that "effectively resulted in a $3.00 per share conversion rate" in Harken common stock seemed fair to them even though the market was currently pricing the common stock at $4.00.[11]

The details of the story are not clear enough to charge anyone with blatant dishonesty. Most people are enough of a moral mix that even rapacious dealmakers who live ruthlessly off the little people may strive to convince themselves otherwise. But the major insiders were, at minimum, giving the interest of the ordinary shareholders no thought. That left open the possibility of plunder just as much as if robbery were intended.

Too low a conversion rate for the new shares would result in an unfairly large stock issue, diluting the value of shares already outstanding. That was of little concern to major shareholders whose profit in the preferred stock would much more than offset any losses they suffered from the diluted value of their common shares. Meanwhile, small shareholders with no preferred stock to trade would suffer a net loss of value in the shares they owned.

Up to this point George Bush had been a cooperative member of the board. He would have been something of an ingrate to have gone looking for trouble at Harken. After all, the company had saved him from his troubles with Spectrum 7 and then paid him a "consulting fee" that left him free to pursue his political interests. He had raised no objections when the dubious Aloha deal went through.

But Bush drew the line at exploitation of small shareholders. He appointed himself defender of the little people in the break-up plan. According to the minutes of the May 11, 1990, board meeting, Bush asserted that a fundamental principle guiding the deal had to be "preservation of value for the small shareholders of the company."[12]

He evidently spoke with effect. The board appointed a three-member committee consisting of Bush, the Harken CEO, and another board member to investigate the fairness of the price for the preferred stock. Major insiders were excluded from membership on this "fairness committee."

On May 17 the fairness committee met with its consultant from Smith Barney and with an additional Harken director representing the Harvard Management Corporation, which ran the Harvard University endowment. Harvard was investing heavily in energy companies and was one of the major shareholders in Harken. The Harvard representative on the Harken board seems to have been the moving spirit in the rights offering.

At the May 17 meeting, the fairness committee was in a strong position to challenge Harvard since, thanks to Bush, the board had gone on record as wanting a fair conversion rate for the preferred stock. The Harken CEO opened the meeting by asking the Smith Barney consultant to discuss the price "proposed by the major shareholders particularly in light of the board's charge to the [Fairness] Committee."[13] This was followed by a back and forth between the Harvard and Smith Barney representatives as to the risks and rewards that would fall to the major shareholders as a result of the rights offering.

Finally, the director from Harvard raised the major shareholders' bid to $4.00 per share, a 33-percent increase over their initial proposal. The minutes show that dilution of value in the common shares—the issue Bush had put on the table—was the main question of the meeting. The Harvard man pointed out that the "$4.00 per share conversion price ... would result in issuance of approximately 7.44 million shares of stock versus the 9.33 million shares which had been projected."[14] In other words, with a conversion rate of $4.00 a share rather than $3.00, the major shareholders would get 1.89 million fewer shares of common stock in return for surrendering their preferred stock.

Even then the deal was not done. Smith Barney needed time to decide if the $4.00 conversion price was fair. Yet on May 17 Harken was down to three days' cash. It took a temporary loan from the major shareholders, secured by Harken assets, to stave off bankruptcy while waiting for Smith Barney's decision on the fairness of the price for the preferred stock.

Nor was that the end of the pressure that Bush had put on Harken by slowing down the rights offering in the interest of fairness. To conserve cash while waiting for approval of the rights offering, Harken was firing as many employees as possible, leaving the remainder overworked and demoralized. The Harken CEO's memos to the board sounded increasingly frazzled.

Finally, in July 1990 Harken accepted the $4.00 offer, once Smith Barney had studied the question and advised that the conversion price was fair.[15] The $4.00 price was subsequently adjusted downward by a few cents. But Bush's good work on behalf of the small shareholders seems to have held firm for the most part. When the spinoff finally took place, Harken issued 6.9 million shares of its own common stock plus some shares in Tejas and E-Z Serve in return for the preferred stock.[16]

Because of Bush's leadership, the major shareholders took a hit of millions of dollars. They got nowhere near the 9.3 million shares of common stock for which they had originally hoped. The common stock they did not get remained in the Harken treasury where it was the property of all shareholders rather than just the major shareholders.

Bush partisans with whom I have discussed this story are invariably pleased by it. They rightly believe that it confirms their notion that George Bush possesses some good values. But this book makes clear why I think Bush also possesses bad values and is more poorly equipped than he needs to be to help his good values prevail over the bad.

Yet I disagree with those among the Bush critics to whom I have told this story and who insist that if he did something good in his business career, his motivation had to be political. Interpreting Bush's presidency as cynically dishonest, his critics believe that his motivation in looking out for Harken's small shareholders can only have been self-interested. He was just making sure, they say, that he did not participate in anything that would wreck the political career he was planning.

It seems more likely to me that Bush was trying to do the right thing. Yes, his motives were impure, as the motives of all of us are. He may have been unconsciously salving his guilt over selling his name to Harken, guarding his political reputation, protecting his self-image, and looking out for himself in countless other ways, just as we all do. But those were not his only motives. He saw a bad thing happening, didn't like it, and did his best to substitute right for wrong.

Sometimes a few good values really are all it takes to make the right decision. If the issue is simple and involves no cost to oneself, it may not be hard to achieve what Bush would later call "moral clarity." Bush's good actions in the rights offering show him possessing enough good values to do the right thing when it is easy to see.

By understanding Bush as possessing values good enough to do the right thing when it's in plain sight, his moral mistakes in more complicated situations become easier to comprehend. Good deeds in simple situations can lay the foundation for false moral confidence in more complex circumstances. Bush's heading off exploitation of Harken's small shareholders could have exacerbated his false pride in his moral leadership.

Without the ability to read Bush's mind, it is impossible to know for certain that such exacerbated false pride contributed a month later to his immoral and probably criminal inside selling of Harken stock, a sale described in chapter 4. But the possibility—likelihood in my view—that heading off others' wrongdoing in the rights offering left him more vulnerable to temptation himself reveals the moral danger in the leadership cult. By protecting small shareholders he seemed to have confirmed the leadership cult's implicit message as to the moral superiority of leaders, leaving himself even less on guard against the risk of self-righteousness.

So as to the goodness of Bush's motives in the Harken rights offering, it seems most reasonable to take the evidence at face value. The minutes of the May 11 meeting show that Bush argued to his fellow board members that they should preserve value for the small shareholders. And they responded by doing the right thing.

Perhaps it would be too strong to say that Bush showed admirable fiduciary responsibility. After all, he only acted the way that directors are supposed to act. Still, Bush's defense of Harken's small shareholders shows that he is right in his estimation of himself as possessing some good values.

Bush's success in this case offers some useful how-to insights on genuine moral leadership in the corporate world. While Bush presumably acted out of a sense of integrity, he never mentioned a code of ethics or a list of company values. If Harken had such paraphernalia, it was ineffective, as the Aloha deal demonstrated. And if it did not have them, there was nothing lost.

Bush succeeded in this case by managing *for* values, not *by* them. The records do not show that Bush ever used the word "value" except in an economic sense. Apparently he acted without self-righteousness, moral pretense, or any discussion of morals at all. Instead of speaking loftily about the value of fairness, he just put it on the table by stating that the board should protect the common shareholders' equity.

Some on the board may have cared little for the common shareholders and perhaps little for Bush by now. A few might have asked themselves, sarcastically, if Bush thought he got his "consulting fee" to serve as company conscience. But the vote in favor of Bush's motion was unanimous, indicating that at minimum no one wanted to go on record as opposing a measure aimed at protecting small shareholders.

Some, maybe many, of the directors probably went along with Bush as a matter of principle. If some of them and, for that matter Bush himself, had previously permitted questionable deals, that did not mean they did not value integrity. They had just not valued it strongly enough to overcome whatever temptations they had faced. Their good values needed to be led, and in this new deal Bush rose to the challenge.

The other directors followed Bush not because he gave them new values but because he appealed to good values that they already held. The cases are few and far between where moral leadership is a matter of choosing and codifying new values for an organization. Moral leadership is usually a matter of managing for already widely accepted values.

Bush also succeeded because he made it a question not just of right and wrong but of competent performance. By calling on his fellow directors to look after the shareholders' interest, he was only asking them to do their jobs. In this case it was easy to see not only the right thing to do but also the connection between integrity and performance.

But moments of moral triumph are also moments of moral danger; they open the way for false pride, a danger which the leadership cult exacerbates. Far more than followers, leaders face the temptations of self-righteousness and moral arrogance, temptations which are heightened both by the leadership cult and by the lack of discipline imposed on leaders from above. It is even easier for leaders than for the rest of us to fall victim to the illusion of being great souls.

It would be fine for any of us to conclude on the basis of our good actions that we are good people if we had well-unified personalities. Unfortunately, even the strongest of us are not perfectly whole. Complex and divided in our thoughts and desires, we are a moral mix, capable of both good and bad.

There is an underlying continuity across time in the emphasis on conflicts and divisions within the human self. Traditional religion emphasizes that the spirit may be willing while the flesh is weak. Depth psychologists have explained our internal conflicts as a division between conscious and unconscious thought. Computers and artificial intelligence have given us the analogy of parallel processing to illustrate why we can simultaneously desire opposing goals, some good, some bad.

In sum, there is no reason for any of us to assume on the basis of our good actions that our values are all good or capable of becoming so. Awareness of our moral imperfection is the fundamental ethical understanding that everyone needs. Leaders need it most of all.

A leader may not have a superior to protect him or her from the moral trap of false pride that can follow a good deed. And of course leaders are exposed to other well-known temptations to moral grandiosity such as adulation, sycophancy, and the simple headiness of power. All these factors compound the moral danger in the leadership cult and its pandering flattery of corporate leaders as moral paragons.

Confronted with such temptations, a leader with some good values still needs all the additional help he or she can get from ethical understanding. A leader who does not understand his or her imperfection and who confidently relies on his or her values underestimates the difficulty of determining and doing the right thing in complex and challenging situations. Such a person may be relatively decent at heart but will not understand the importance of self-examination or of being on guard against false confidence in his or her own values for moral guidance.

Without the ability to read Bush's mind, it is not possible to say that he succumbed to these exact dangers. But he may have, and they are dangers consistent with the leadership cult. Within weeks of his exemplary moral leadership of the Harken board, George Bush engaged in a morally mistaken stock sale.

Chapter 4

A Moral Mistake at Harken Energy

In early June 1990, about a month after Bush admirably defended the Harken small shareholders, he got a call from a Houston stockbroker. The broker had a client who wanted to buy more than 200,000 shares of Harken stock. Bush, who owned more than 300,000 shares, replied that he was interested but needed to think it over.

One question Bush needed to consider was whether it was legal for him to sell. As a Harken director, he had negative inside information that the investing public did not. If that negative inside information was "material"—i.e., important enough that a reasonable outsider would want to have known the same thing before making a buy or sell decision—it was illegal for Bush to sell.

Bush sought the opinion of the Harken general counsel. Although this lawyer later told the SEC that he thought it was legal for Bush to sell, he may have been uneasy about the transaction. He told Bush that he wanted to consult with Harken's outside counsel, the Dallas firm of Haynes and Boone.

The Haynes and Boone opinion arrived on June 15. It advised that any Harken director who sold in advance of the rights offering would risk violating the insider trading laws. The decisive factor, according to Haynes and Boone, was whether positive information outweighed negative: "Unless the favorable facts clearly are more important than the unfavorable, the insider should be advised not to sell."[1]

In short, if the unfavorable information available to Bush as an insider outweighed the favorable, it was wrong for him to sell. This chapter will show that Bush's inside information was overwhelmingly negative. He was wrong to sell his stock.

Bush later defended his sale by arguing that the Bahrain contract meant that he was "selling into good news."[2] But since the public already knew about the Bahrain project, it was irrelevant to the question of whether it was legal for Bush to sell. The question was what inside information he had that outsiders did not.

One major fact that Bush knew and outsiders did not was that Harken might not be around long enough to drill in Bahrain. Much depended on the yet-to-be-priced rights offering. If the deal fell through, Harken could go bankrupt. In that case, Bush's stock sale would look terribly suspicious, which was probably why Haynes and Boone warned that any director who sold in advance of the rights offering risked violating the insider trading laws.

In other words, it was impossible for Bush to know exactly what legal risk he would be taking if he sold. Only later, after Harken either survived because of the rights offering's success or went bankrupt because of its failure, would it be clear whether or not a stock sale would make Bush look like a captain who abandoned ship with his crew still aboard. To sell under such circumstances would be, at minimum, reckless.

The situation hardly met the Haynes and Boone criterion for legal inside selling. Favorable facts did not "clearly" outweigh the unfavorable. To sell would be to risk prison. For sure, it would violate Bush's moral obligation to ordinary shareholders and prospective investors to share their fate until they had all the material information he already possessed.

Yet Bush sold. On June 22, 1990, he accepted the anonymous buyer's offer of $4.00 a share for 212,140 shares of Harken. The sale netted him $848,560.

Just two months after Bush's stock sale, the ground began to shift under him, began to reveal how wrongly he had acted. On August 20, 1990, Harken announced a second quarter loss of $23.2 million. In addition to an operating loss of $6.7 million dollars, the $23 million loss came mostly from cleaning up old messes such as a $2 million restructuring charge to shut down the money-losing trading operation at Harken Marketing.

The most costly item in Harken's second quarter 1990 loss was a $7 million dollar write-down due to the 1989 Aloha deal. Chapter 3 told how Harken had sold Aloha, a chain of Hawaiian gas stations, to IMR, a shell company of Harken insiders. In return Harken got $1 million in cash and an $11 million note from IMR. Subsequently, IMR sold

Aloha to another company, Advance Petroleum, and as part of the deal passed on the $11 million obligation to Harken.

Declining oil prices provoked fear at Harken that Advance would default on the $11 million debt. To add to its woes, Harken retained liability for clean-up costs of Aloha's leaky underground gasoline tanks. It looked like the cleanup could be unexpectedly costly at just the time when Harken was in a liquidity crisis.

So Harken had made a deal with Advance that raised cash but damaged Harken's balance sheet. Advance paid Harken $1 million, agreed to accelerate payments on the note, and assumed Harken's responsibility for environmental damage from Aloha's leaky underground gasoline tanks. In return, Harken lowered the note's balance and interest rate, forcing a write-down on the balance sheet of what had been an $11 million asset by $7.2 million.[3] The Aloha deal had come home to roost.

The announcement of the $23 million quarterly loss put Harken's share price in free fall. Just prior to the August 20 loss announcement, Harken shares had been at $3.00, down $1.00 from the $4.00 price at which Bush sold in June. On August 20, the day that the company announced its $23 million loss, Harken's share price tumbled in a few hours from $3.00 to $2-3/8 (stocks were still priced in fractions rather than decimals in 1990). By the end of the year, Harken was at $1-1/2.

If outside investors had known that Bush got out at $4.00 in June, his inside selling could have made some of them want to do the same. But outsiders had been deprived of timely information on Bush's sale. He did not report the transaction to the SEC until early March 1991, eight months after the legal deadline.[4]

Bush's explanation for the late filing changed over the years. First, he claimed that he had filed on time but that the SEC had lost the paperwork. Later, he said his lawyer had meant to file the document but misplaced it.[5]

The latter seems more likely. In an earlier, unrelated incident Bush had filed an insider trading report late because of the company lawyer's illness.[6] Bush seems to have tolerated carelessness in such matters. The SEC later found that he had violated reporting requirements for inside trades on four occasions.[7]

Bush's latest violation of the reporting laws, coinciding with Harken's huge second quarter loss for 1990, prompted an SEC investigation. Although Bush's father had the year before moved into the mansion at 1600 Pennsylvania Avenue, the SEC officials who conducted the investigation may have really tried to ensure that Bush got the same treatment as anyone else. An SEC political appointee and friend of the Bush family recused himself from the investigation.

The SEC eventually decided not to refer Bush's case to the Justice Department for a criminal investigation. And the SEC's Enforcement Division seemed unembarrassed by that outcome. It subsequently briefed a congressional oversight committee, controlled by Democrats, on the Bush investigation and its findings.[8]

Yet even though there is no hard evidence of favoritism toward Bush, the fact is that the SEC investigation lacked thoroughness. This chapter will show that the SEC's conclusion that "it appears that Bush did not engage in illegal insider trading"[9] was wrong. From the available evidence, "it appears" that Bush broke the law. The SEC should have turned Bush's case over to the Justice Department for a criminal investigation and possible prosecution.

But even without a criminal investigation, Bush's case makes a useful study in business ethics. The case shows how difficult it can be for a person who seems to rely only on his or her own values to tell right from wrong, especially when self-interest is at stake. It therefore also shows how wrong the leadership cult is to promote such reliance on values.

The records are too thin for this chapter to prove conclusively that the cult of moral leadership directly caused Bush's stock sale. But by supporting excessive moral confidence and failing to provide real ethical understanding, the leadership cult makes such moral errors more likely. Relying on his values and lacking ethical understanding as to how difficult it is to achieve moral self-knowledge, Bush was probably far less on guard than he needed to be against self-deception and self-righteousness.

Bush may have been especially susceptible to self-righteousness in June 1990 since, in May, he seemed to have proven himself a moral leader by defending Harken's small shareholders during the planning for the rights offering. A month later, facing temptation, he needed the teaching of traditional moralists that good deeds can lead to false pride. He may never even have considered the possibility that he might be bested by temptation.

One temptation that could have been at work on Bush was a desire to begin to exit Harken. Continuing his association with so ethically challenged a company could destroy his chances at the political career he wanted. If voters ever learned of Harken's sketchy deals, they might not have understood that Bush had sometimes played the role of good guy, had sometimes protected the small shareholders.

Bush had a politically preferable place to work thanks to his 1989 purchase of a share in the Texas Rangers baseball team where he had a leadership role and was making himself the public face of the club. With his eye on the Texas governorship, the Rangers offered him a way to answer the voters' question, "What's he done?" Giving the fans a winning team and having his picture taken with Nolan Ryan would make Bush more electable than hanging on at Harken.

The Rangers deal created another tempting reason for Bush to sell his Harken stock. He was eager to pay back the $600,000 he had borrowed to purchase his share in the ball club. One of his attorneys later told SEC investigators that Bush's financial advisor—it sounds as if the lawyer was quoting Bush verbatim—had been "bugging him to get liquid."[10]

So even before the broker called with the offer for most of his Harken stock, Bush was selling his shares in other companies. He parted with $337,000 worth of Greenwich Financial on June 8 and, on June 13, $73,000 worth of America Waste Systems. By mid-July 1990 Bush had sold more than $600,000 of his non-Harken holdings. But he had to use a third of the money raised by those stock sales to pay a $200,000 tax bill.[11] To get entirely out from under his Texas Rangers debt, Bush needed to take the offer for his Harken shares.

Still another tempting factor may have been the sheer size of the offer for Bush's Harken stock. Harken was a relatively small company that traded in tens of thousands of shares a day or even less. Buyers for large blocks of Harken stock were few and far between. If Bush rejected the offer and later put 200,000 shares on the open market, the price might collapse.

To these considerable temptations, Bush probably made no conscious surrender. Like most of us mortals, he invests energy in being able to think well of himself. He probably did not say to himself that he was going to do something that was likely illegal and certainly wrong.

More likely, Bush convinced himself that it was all right to sell. As explained later in this chapter, his method of self-justification was probably not psychological rationalization. His method was probably psychological denial of the importance of the negative inside information he possessed.

That Bush should have concluded differently—should have decided it was wrong to sell—is clear from facts turned up in the later SEC investigation. Those facts are small as well as large. For contrary to what one would have expected from the Haynes and Boone memo, the SEC ignored the rights offering as well as Harken's financial fragility and risk of bankruptcy. Instead, the SEC investigated lesser issues that nevertheless revealed how wrong Bush was to sell.

SEC investigators gave three specific reasons for their conclusion that Bush appeared to have broken no law:

(1) the evidence indicates that Bush did not have advance notice of most of the information contained in Harken's August 20, 1990, earnings announcement when he sold on June 22;

(2) Bush's conduct prior to his June 22 sale, including consultation with attorneys and Harken's CEO, would make it difficult to establish that he acted with scienter when he sold his Harken stock; and

(3) the market's reaction to Harken's August 20 earnings announcement could make it difficult to prove that the market considered that announcement to be material.[12]

Unfortunately, SEC officials missed, omitted, or failed to investigate available evidence working against all three of the reasons stated above.

In support of their first point—Bush's supposed ignorance of most of Harken's impending loss when he sold—SEC investigators said that he was "not aware of ... expenses associated ... with a restructuring efforts [sic]" at Harken Marketing that "occurred after June 22."[13] Yet the SEC possessed minutes of the May 11 Harken board meeting which Bush attended (it was the meeting at which he had spoken up for the small shareholders in the rights offering). At that meeting, the Harken directors "discussed at length the supply and trading operations of HMC [Harken Marketing]," deliberated on "the most appropriate means of eliminating these activities," and decided "to develope [sic] a written plan to wind down the supply and trading operation."[14]

Therefore, the only thing Bush may not have known about the restructuring when he sold on June 22 was its exact cost, which was not announced till August 20. But his presence at the May 11 meeting can leave no doubt as to his understanding that the restructuring was a complex and major issue. Bush had to have known—and outsiders did not—that the restructuring would be costly.

The SEC took a similar position on Bush's knowledge of the $7 million Aloha write-down. He could not have known, the investigators said, of the impending loss on the Aloha note when he sold on June 22 because "Harken management was not aware of the accounting effects of the Aloha transaction until mid-July 1990 at the earliest."[15] But in fact, the SEC had notes in its files from Harken's Executive Committee meeting on May 14—more than a month in advance of Bush's stock sale—estimating that the Aloha write-down would involve a "resulting loss of $3 million."[16] That estimate was less than half of what the Aloha loss came to in the end, but it still showed that the SEC was wrong. Harken management understood in May, not July, that the Aloha the loss would be large for a company of its size.

Even if the SEC had not possessed evidence to the contrary, its statement that Harken management did not understand until mid-July the accounting implications of restructuring the Aloha note was not credible. A first-year accounting student would have understood that reducing either the note's balance or interest rate—Harken was doing both— would negatively affect the balance sheet. And a drop in balance sheet assets could only be accounted for by reducing the income statement.

Bush was not a member of the executive committee and therefore did not attend the May 14 meeting where the loss from renegotiating the Aloha note was estimated at $3 million. But he was present at the earlier, March 14 board meeting where the directors, including him, voted to authorize Harken's president to renegotiate the Aloha note.[17] Bush could certainly not have imagined that the Aloha note would be renegotiated on terms favorable to Harken. He knew that renegotiating the note would be costly.

In short, evidence in the SEC's files contradicts its first reason for not referring Bush's case to the Justice Department—his supposed ignorance of most of the factors causing the second quarter loss as well as the supposed unimportance of what he did know. Bush knew that Harken Marketing was being restructured and that the Aloha note was being renegotiated. And he knew that those actions would be costly even if he did not know the exact dollar amounts. Outside investors would have considered such information important, and that was all it should have taken for Bush to realize it was wrong to sell.

The SEC's second argument against referring Bush's case to the Justice Department for a criminal investigation was that it would have been difficult to convict him of a crime. According to the SEC, Bush's seeking of legal advice would have made it difficult to prove that he acted with *scienter*, or criminal intent. But the SEC investigators reached that conclusion without knowing what legal advice Bush actually received. Although the SEC requested a copy of the Haynes and Boone written opinion, it closed Bush's case just one day before the copy arrived at its Washington office![18]

The SEC simply accepted the Bush lawyers' word for it as to what Haynes and Boone advised. Bush and Harken both waived attorney-client privilege, allowing the Harken lawyer to tell the SEC that "Haynes and Boone ... saw no reason why Bush could not sell his stock."[19] And Bush's personal lawyer also told the SEC that Haynes and Boone "saw no reason why Bush could not sell his shares."[20]

It is interesting that Bush's personal attorney and the Harken lawyer used identical words to summarize the Haynes and Boone opinion to the SEC. It is literally true that Haynes and Boone "saw no reason why Bush could not sell." But the truth of those words depended on the fact that Haynes and Boone, after advising of a special risk in selling ahead of the rights offering, had left it up to Bush to decide whether "the favorable facts clearly are more important than the unfavorable."[21] Bush's attorney and the Harken lawyer could just as accurately have told the SEC that Haynes and Boone saw no reason why Bush *could* sell.

The SEC may therefore have been wrong in its idea that Bush's consulting a lawyer would have made it difficult to establish criminal intent. If Bush knew of Haynes and Boone's advice not to sell if bad news outweighed good, he acted against the legal advice he received. And if he sold without waiting for the Haynes and Boone opinion, he disregarded the Harken lawyer's advice that an outside opinion was needed.

It is possible, however, that the Haynes and Boone memo might have worked to Bush's advantage had he stood trial. The Harken lawyer, according to the SEC, told investigators that he "conveyed the results of his conversations with Haynes and Boone ... to Bush and told Bush that he was free to sell his stock."[22] If that is true, Bush might have been able to argue in his defense that the Harken lawyer advised him that Haynes and Boone believed it was legal to sell.

But if the SEC had not closed the case without at least waiting to see the actual Haynes and Boone memo, it would have known that it was not clear what legal advice Bush received. Haynes and Boone warned not to sell in the face of inside information that was more bad than good, and Bush's inside information was overwhelmingly bad. The actual Haynes and Boone memo, therefore, seems to be in conflict with the Harken lawyer's advice to Bush, as reported by the SEC, that Haynes and Boone considered him "free to sell." There was enough mixed and contradictory evidence to have justified further investigation by the Justice Department as to what legal advice Bush actually received.

Moreover, the information the SEC did have as to the legal advice Bush received was obtained under his waiver of attorney-client privilege. Bush's legal advice might, therefore, have been admissible as evidence in a trial. Contrary to the SEC's idea that Bush's consulting a lawyer provided a defense against *scienter* or criminal intent, a prosecutor might have convinced a jury that Bush acted against the advice he received.

Additionally, there is the question whether a director with inside information that his company was inches away from bankruptcy really needed a lawyer's opinion to know it was illegal to sell. Consulting a lawyer does not make it all right to commit an obvious crime. A prosecutor might well have convinced a jury that whatever legal advice Bush got was irrelevant in so clear a matter. A jury might have concluded that if Bush got bad legal advice it was because he was seeking it—that is, he was seeking cover for a sale that any corporate director should have known was illegal.

So the SEC's second reason for not referring Bush's case to the Justice Department—that Bush's consulting a lawyer would have made it hard to convict him—does not stand. The SEC did not know what advice Bush received. And in any case, a director should have needed no legal advice to know it was wrong to sell when outsiders did not know that Harken was nearly bankrupt. Bush's consulting a lawyer might have served as evidence for, not against, *scienter*.

The SEC's third reason for concluding that there was insufficient evidence to prosecute Bush was that "investors did not view ... as material information" Harken's August 20 announcement of its $23 million loss in the second quarter of 1990. The SEC analyst based her opinion on two facts. First, Harken's price held firm for several hours after the announcement before falling from $3.00 to $2-3/8. Second, the stock price briefly recovered to $3.00 the next day.

The SEC analyst argued that "the failure of Harken's stock price to move immediately following the earnings announcement ... weakens the link ... [to] Harken's price drop."[23] She cited an academic paper as the basis of her opinion that "stock prices usually incorporate earnings information within 5 to 10 minutes." That academic paper was based on a study of 96 firms large enough to "guarantee a close following by analysts."[24]

It is unlikely, however, that Harken had a "close following by analysts." Harken had been growing rapidly through acquisitions, but it was still not a major oil company and was not heavily traded. News about it might have moved more slowly and taken longer to reach interested people than news about the companies on which the academic study cited by the SEC was based.

The SEC analyst also contradicted herself on the significance of time gaps between Harken's loss announcement and movements in its stock price. First, she said that a gap of several hours *weakened* the link between the August 20 announcement and the price drop. But she also argued that the stock's price recovery 24 hours later "*strengthens* the argument against [the loss announcement's] materiality."[25]

The SEC analyst admitted that "If viewed by itself, the 23 percent stock price drop over August 20 is large and statistically significant." But the price recovery the next day suggested "that investors overreacted to the earnings announcement, recognized their error, and corrected it. Such price reversals are rare, but not unheard of."[26]

The SEC analyst admitted that her argument would not hold if "another reason exists for the price rebound on August 21."[27] And another possible reason did exist—the Bahrain contract. Speculators wanting to bet on the Bahrain project could have seen the drop in Harken's share price on August 20 as a buying opportunity. In other words, some investors could have seen the loss announcement as material and sold Harken shares, lowering the price, only to have others speculatively bid the price back up the next day.

It had not taken much selling to lower Harken's share price on August 20, and it did not take much buying to restore it on August 21. The SEC probably had the trading records, but the report made no mention of the fact that Harken traded thinly. Here is the volume for August 20, the day of the loss announcement, and for the two trading days on either side:

Date	Number of Shares Traded[28]
August 16	6,000
August 17	22,300
August 20	30,800
August 21	77,300
August 22	53,000

No zeroes have been dropped. Harken trading was in tens of thousands of shares a day or even less. And its price range during that time was $2-3/8 to $3.00 per share. A few buyers, or even just one, could have bought all the shares sold on August 21 for around $200,000, bidding Harken back up to $3.00 in the process. What the SEC analyst interpreted as a broad market correction could have reflected the actions of one or a handful of speculators while other investors continued to see the loss announcement as material.

Moreover, the SEC either ignored or missed evidence in its possession contradicting its idea that investors were concerned for a day at most about the August 20 loss announcement. In an August 27 memo, the Harken president reported to directors that he had "received many calls (brokers, investment bankers, shareholders, industry partners, creditors, etc.) as a result of the news release" announcing the $23 million loss. Only when he wrote, on August 27, did the Harken president believe the situation had "stabilized."[29]

So the SEC's third reason for not referring the case to the Justice Department for a criminal investigation does not stand. The SEC's idea that investors were not concerned by the $23 million second quarter loss ignored evidence to the contrary. And the SEC's conclusion also rested on academic opinion about price movements that may not have been appropriate for so thinly traded a company as Harken.

In sum, all three of the SEC's reasons for not referring Bush's case to the Justice Department do not survive close examination. First, the SEC investigation was not thorough enough either to discover all of what Bush knew on June 22 or to determine the materiality of the information that he is known to have possessed. Second, evidence available to the SEC relating to Bush's legal advice, far from clearing him, might have supported a prosecutor's argument that Bush acted with criminal intent. And third, some investors were deeply concerned by the $23 million second quarter loss and saw it as very material.

The SEC should have referred the case to the Justice Department. If the case had gone to trial, even George Bush might have found it no easy matter to stay out of prison. And a trial would have aired enough of the story that even if there had been an acquittal, we would surely have been spared Bush's presidency.

For regardless of whether or not Bush could have been convicted of a crime, the records of the case leave no doubt that he acted wrongly. The complexity of the evidence presented in this chapter should not obscure the basic fact that Bush violated his moral obligation to share the fate of outsiders as long as he had material inside information that they did not. Only when those people knew what Bush knew would it have been all right for him to sell.

Instead, Bush betrayed ordinary shareholders and prospective buyers by selling while possessing material inside information. He knew that Harken was on the edge of bankruptcy while outsiders did not. He knew that Harken Marketing was undergoing a costly restructuring while outsiders did not. And he knew that the Aloha note was being renegotiated at a loss while outsiders did not. His stock sale was probably criminal and, for certain, immoral.

It would have cost Bush money to have done the right thing by refusing to sell at $4 in June. If he had waited until August 20 when the loss announcement drove Harken down to $2-3/8, he would have received $290,000 less for his stock. Even after the price recovered on August 21 to $3.00, the highest price for the rest of 1990, he would have gotten $212,000 less. By year's end the price had slid to $1-1/2, at which point Bush would have got $530,000 less. And those numbers presume that he could have put a huge block of shares on the market without driving the price down further.

Bush's hundreds of thousands of dollars of extra profit did not come out of thin air. It came at the expense of the buyer of his stock. The *Boston Globe* has identified the most likely buyer as Quest Advisory, an investment firm specializing in distressed companies.[30] But did Quest know exactly how distressed Harken was? The inside trading laws are meant to protect outsiders like Quest from insiders like Bush.

For business ethics it is an interesting question how a person as committed as Bush seems to be to maintaining a righteous self-image could have justified such an act. Given the situational knowledge available to Bush, it would have taken strenuous rationalization for him to have reconciled his stock sale with his vaunted values. If he went through a process of psychological justification, that process was probably not rationalization but denial.

Psychological denial could have helped Bush maintain a simplistic self-image as a man of good values rather than recognize that in this instance his actions indicated that he valued money more than his duty. Denial would have helped him avoid seeing the implications for Harken's stock price and income statement of restructuring HMC and renegotiating the Aloha note. As opposed to a complex process of rationalization, all that psychological denial required of him was failure to connect the dots.

If Bush did engage in psychological denial, it could have been helped by his lack of ethical understanding as to the importance of supporting whatever good values he possessed with moral caution and self-examination. Overly confident in his values as a guide for ethical decisions, he may also have been at that moment in time especially vulnerable to self-righteousness resulting from his holding up of the rights offering just a month earlier. Bush seemed to have shown then that he was a moral leader with good values.

From the perspective of this book's argument about the danger of the leadership cult, it is ultimately less important that Bush acted wrongly than that he probably had no idea he had done so. If he had gone to jail, he would probably have been just as mystified as was Ken Lay as to how he could have deserved such a fate. Whether or not Bush belongs in the big house instead of the White House, his actions are consistent with the leadership cult that blinded Lay and many other corporate felons to their wrongdoing.

Even with the perspective of time, Bush probably looked back on his stock sale with no qualms of conscience, no understanding that he had probably acted criminally and for certain immorally. In self-justification, he could recall that he had consulted lawyers. If he ignored legal advice or if he got bad advice, that was a small point. After all, he had survived an SEC investigation.

With his conscience clean, Bush may have been reassured that his values gave him all the moral clarity he needed. Because of an inadequate SEC investigation, he had missed what was probably the best chance of his life to learn not just theoretically but practically that good values do not preclude bad. Even more than before his morally mistaken stock sale, Bush would have been able to believe that he was the stuff of which moral leaders are made.

Chapter 5

The Ethics of Leadership

Would a better understanding of ethics have helped George Bush avoid his moral mistake in selling his Harken stock while possessing important inside information? Maybe. Maybe not. Just as having some good values does not guarantee good deeds, neither does knowing some moral philosophy.

Still, Bush relied mainly on his values when he wrongly sold his Harken shares. He might have done better with more ethical understanding. The knowledge that it is not possible to know for certain what we value might have helped him to achieve more moral caution on the question of whether it was all right to sell.

In other words, Bush might have profited from understanding that we live in a morally dangerous world where it is easy for fallible human beings to slip up without even knowing it. Of course he probably believes that he already understands quite well the moral imperfection of humanity and its orb. That, after all, is one of the essential teachings of his Christian faith.

And it is not just Christianity which holds that we and our world could use a lot of improvement. All of the major religions teach that we live in a morally imperfect world and that we share in its moral imperfection. This common ethical doctrine of the world's religions is incontestable to anyone who stops to reflect on it. George Bush undoubtedly possesses, at minimum, a Sunday School conviction that we are all sinners.

But part of our sinfulness lies in our tendency to forget our moral imperfections when we're not in churches, temples, and mosques. That is why the unrealistic moral optimism in the leadership cult is so dangerous. It heightens the risk that leaders' holy-day humility will swell into weekday grandiosity.

At the same time that leaders may be misled by the leadership cult, they are also more exposed than the rest of us to morally enervating forces such as power, perquisites, and sycophancy. Yet leaders can afford moral enervation even less than the rest of us. Leaders are exposed to more character-corrupting forces than the rest of us while they also have more opportunities to practice corruption.

Leading, in short, is a morally dangerous activity. Yet we need and want effective leaders, without whom we are far less likely to achieve our goals. That our well-being depends on so morally ambiguous an activity as leadership is one more indicator of the world's moral imperfection.

Still worse, it is a fair question whether leaders, wielding the power that they do, may not best succeed by a judicious balance of morality and immorality. Machiavelli (1469–1527) became the greatest writer on the exercise of power by deciding "to go after the real truth of the matter rather than what people have imagined."[1] He concluded that the prince—and by extension the corporate executive—can best succeed by sometimes being "a great liar and hypocrite."[2] So skillfully did Machiavelli argue for the usefulness of mendacity in a prince that he performed the considerable service of showing how difficult it is to be a genuinely moral leader.

Upright and honorable in his personal life, Machiavelli would have preferred not to be a Machiavellian. But he had to work with the material at hand. Florence in his time had fallen into decline and was governed despotically. So he wrote his great book, *The Prince*, in the hope that a well-advised tyrant could lead a turnaround.

The Prince is germane to the exercise of power in all fields but is especially relevant to business leadership today. Despite the guru-speak of bottom-up empowerment, modern CEOs bear some resemblance to renaissance princes. There is a difference, of course, in that executives, unlike princes, seldom inherit their jobs by birth. But like princes and unlike democratic leaders, corporate managers can dismiss those below them, not vice versa.

Executives confident that their powerful positions are indications of righteousness ought to take caution from Machiavelli's advice. The Florentine philosopher argued that a prince who tries to rule strictly by good methods "is bound to come to ruin among the great number [of people] who are not good."[3] Therefore, "something resembling virtue, if you follow it, may be your ruin, while something else resembling vice will lead, if you follow it, to your security and well being."[4] In other words, what would be vice for others may be virtue for a prince.

The chance that Machiavelli was right is only enhanced by the fact that when he got down to specifics, he had good practical advice for leaders. Every teacher who has ever had an unruly class understands the wisdom of Machiavelli's insistence that top-down authority must be maintained with a strong hand. Since regaining control may require harsh measures, rulers who are firm in the first place are really kinder "than those who, in their tenderheartedness, allow disorders to occur."[5]

We blanch at Machiavelli's idea that "to be feared is much safer than to be loved."[6] But this was only an honest acknowledgment that effective use of top-down power inspires fear in the ranks. It is foolish and dishonest for the powerful to deny that "dread of punishment" can be useful in managing their subordinates.[7]

Yet Machiavelli knew that followers' respect is the key to leadership. Hence his advice that while fear has its uses, hatred does not. A prince who is hated rather than respected by his followers must rule by force alone and therefore falls when weak.

The prince can gain respect by accomplishing not just his goals but the people's. Whatever one thinks of Machiavelli's ethics, there is no denying that he was right to remind leaders that ultimately they are judged by results. The way for a prince to gain his people's respect is to "win victories, and uphold his state."[8]

To avoid losing respect while achieving results through wrongdoing, the prince should cover his dishonesty with a façade of morality. The few to whom the prince is unjust will be helpless against the many who are deceived by his moral pretense. Therefore, the prince "should appear all compassion, all honor, all humanity, all integrity, all religion." Of "this last virtue"—religion—Machiavelli said that "Nothing is more necessary than to seem to have it."[9]

Clearly, Machiavelli's argument is not good news for those who aspire to moral leadership. But it would be foolish to deny that, just as Machiavelli said, corrupt leaders can and not infrequently do succeed, not just for a moment but for a lifetime. The fact that dishonesty can get results is a major reason why even leaders who in general want to do the right thing can be tempted into moral errors in particular situations. That may have been the case with George Bush in his morally mistaken stock sale.

Against moral danger so murky, good values can only be our first line of defense. We need not only values but ethical understanding. By recognizing that it is sometimes difficult to do right and easy to err, we can better guard against unwitting surrender to our bad values and against slipping unawares into Machiavellianism. By thinking hard about ethics, we can also ask if the moral situation of leaders is quite as black as Machiavelli painted it.

Machiavelli runs counter to one of the great western traditions in moral philosophy—virtue ethics. Aristotle (384–22 BCE), the founder of this tradition, said that virtue "is the result of habit or custom."[10] On the basis of personal experience, most of us will agree with Aristotle that the more habitual a virtue or a vice becomes, the easier it is to repeat it.

Yet Machiavelli's focus on government allows a sort of practical and temporary compromise with Aristotle's focus on personal virtue. The Greek philosopher said that to possess the virtue of honesty a person should live neither corruptly (a deficiency of honesty) nor punctiliously (an excess of honesty). Rather, the virtue of honesty is achieved by living in a middle ground or "golden mean" of integrity. And that golden mean, according to Aristotle, will fall at a somewhat different place for each of us depending on our innate characters and dispositions.

In other words, Aristotle focuses on the individual and sees virtue as a matter of what will most fully develop the individual's character. Aristotle pays less attention to abstract principles of duty or of community obligation than did later philosophers. A prince could conceivably practice Aristotelian ethics on issues that seem close to his personal identity and Machiavellian ethics on questions that seem more connected to duty and community.

For example, Bush in his face-to-face dealings with fellow board members at Harken Energy might have been moved by an Aristotelian sense of integrity and a strong desire to preserve his personal character. But in subsequently selling his stock through a broker, it may have been easier for him to disregard his duty to remote shareholders and investors. Because Bush seems to think of ethics in personal terms as mainly a matter of values, more abstract issues of duty may be more of a challenge for him.

In short, George Bush represents the possible co-existence of Aristotelian and Machiavellian impulses in a leader. With his focus on his personal behavior and on good values, Bush is a sort of Aristotelian virtue ethicist, though it is probably a safe bet he does not know it. And his morally mistaken but profitable sale of Harken stock indicates a possible Machiavellianism.

If Aristotle does not offer a perfect counter to Machiavelli, might a better answer reside in a different tradition in moral philosophy, the deontological ethics of Immanuel Kant (1724–1804)? The difference between Aristotle and Kant is that the former focused on personal virtue and the latter on duty. To follow Kantian ethics is to focus less on developing a good character than on figuring out what one should do and then doing it.

Good will, according to Kant, is the best thing in the world and the more of it the better. Therefore, one's duty is to will and to do what is best for the whole world, which leads to his "categorical imperative." One should "Act only on that maxim through which you can at the same time will that it should become a universal law."[11]

For instance, lying may be to my advantage. But the gain I get from lying would be more than offset if everyone else felt free, in Kant's words, to "pay me back in like coin."[12] Therefore, I can truly will that veracity should be a universal law, which means that I should not lie.

In addition, Kant argued that there is a practical imperative of "respect for persons." Kant believed we show respect for others by treating them "never simply as a means, but always as an end."[13] While it is often necessary to use other people—employees, for example—to achieve our business goals, we should treat them as more than means to our ends. We should respect other people as ends in themselves.

Kant based his argument for these duties on the premise of a rational universe, a metaphysical assumption that some philosophers reject today. And many commentators have observed that in specific, real life situations, Kant's abstractly stated principles are much more difficult to apply than he seemed to think. Still, many people will intuitively agree with Kant that we should

1. act out of good will toward the whole world;
2. act in a way that we would be willing for everyone else to act;
3. treat other people as ends in themselves, not just as a means to achieve our own goals.

More clearly than any other philosopher, Kant tells us what is morally wrong in Machiavelli. By deceiving his subjects when he perceives it to be to his advantage, the prince violates the categorical imperative to act in a way that he would be willing for all others to act. And when the prince treats others wrongly for reasons of state, he violates the imperative of respect for persons, the duty to treat other people as ends in themselves.

But Machiavellians could well reply to the latter point by arguing that there is a practical problem with Kant's principle of respect for persons. It is often impossible for real-world princes and managers to treat every person as an end in himself or herself. Organizational leaders exercise power at a distance, which often makes it impossible to treat other people as ends, not means.

For example, a business leader may make a decision on downsizing or outsourcing that means dismissing a large number of employees. A severance package may reflect the leader's good will. But it scarcely means that the leader has weighed the situation of every employee to see if severance is good for each person considered as an end in himself or herself.

In other words, some degree of immorality in the form of disrespect for persons is an inescapable part of organizational leadership. Organizations, which improve life in general, make it impossible to consider the needs of every person in particular. Human beings have rightly chosen the material benefits of organizational life over Kantian moral purity. But in doing so, we have accepted the necessity of some degree of Machiavellian immorality.

Yet even if Machiavelli is right in a practical sense that vices can be virtues in princes, vices are still vices by Kant's absolute standards. If Kant cannot save organizational leaders from necessarily practicing some immorality, he can at least warn them that some degree of immorality is built into their jobs. And it is no small thing for the CEO of a company or the president of a country to understand that they are inevitably immoral leaders to some degree. That knowledge may put them on guard morally and help them to minimize their wrongdoing.

But even though Kant's ideas are useful for teaching organizational leaders the importance of moral caution, they are too abstract to serve as a realistic guide for organizational life where sometimes leaders must either disrespect persons or act as we would not wish all others to act. Kantian ethics are therefore a mixed success at best in answering Machiavelli's arguments for princely immorality. Machiavelli's ideas, just as he claimed, seem more realistic.

What about the third great tradition in western moral philosophy, the utilitarian ethics of Jeremy Bentham (1748–1832)? Rather than concerning himself with Aristotelian virtue or Kantian duty, Bentham judged an action good or bad depending on its utility, its effect. An action is good if its tendency "to augment the happiness of the community is greater than any which it has to diminish it."[14]

Bentham's urging us to pay attention to the effect of our actions on others can be a useful corrective to Aristotle and Kant. There is a risk of self-centeredness in Aristotle's virtue ethics and even in Kant's categorical imperative. To focus on improving our character or on doing our duty runs the risk of losing sight of the help or harm we do to other people.

But good as Bentham's principle of utility is for all of us, including leaders, it does not refute Machiavelli. The Florentine philosopher believed that a ruthless and hypocritical prince was more likely to increase the well-being of the community than a ruler who strives for personal virtue. Utilitarian ethics therefore pose no difficulty for Machiavelli.

There is one more way in which the major moral philosophers not only fail to refute Machiavelli but actually provide support for him. The ethics of Aristotle, Kant, and Bentham sometimes conflict. To follow, say, Bentham by acting in the interest of the majority may fatally injure the minority, thereby violating Kant's principle that persons are to be treated as ends in themselves.

For example, when Bush attacked Iraq, he killed innocent people and thereby violated the Kantian duty always to respect persons. When you kill people you can scarcely claim to have treated them as ends in themselves. Yet if fear of weapons of mass destruction (WMDs) was his motive, as Bush claimed, then he acted morally according to the Benthamite principle of the greatest good for the greatest number. He was trying to prevent a proven mass murderer from killing even more innocent people than Bush killed in his preemptive attack.

Since Saddam Hussein had no WMDs, Bush turns out to have been wrong not only by the Kantian standard of respect for persons but by the Benthamite principle of the greatest good for the greatest number. Innocent people died unnecessarily, even by utilitarian standards. Bush's terrible error illustrates the importance not just of personal values but of situational knowledge and professional competence in making moral decisions.

But if there really had been WMDs in Iraq, Bush's situation would have exemplified the dilemma of a leader who must choose between respecting persons or acting for the greater good. To have respected persons by not invading might have led to greater carnage in the future. But to accomplish the greater good of preventing that carnage would have required the disrespecting of innocent people by killing them, albeit unintentionally, in the course of the attack.

In short, there are decisions in which it is impossible to uphold one ethical standard without violating another. Some of the most wrenching ethical decisions are not between right and wrong. They are between right and right.

This conflict between different ethical systems, each of which seems reasonable when considered alone, is one more piece of evidence as to the world's moral imperfection. It lends support to Machiavelli's insistence that the real world is too morally mixed a place for a consistently moral leader to prevail or, more accurately for there to be such a thing as a consistently moral leader.

I regret that I do not know enough of non-western traditions in ethics—Confucianism for example—to search there for an answer to the Florentine philosopher. But Machiavelli's moral pessimism seems to be a reasonably realistic response to the world's moral imperfection. I am therefore skeptical that non-western traditions could improve much on the inadequate answers to Machiavelli in Aristotle, Kant, and Bentham.

Yet if the moral philosophers do not completely refute Machiavelli, they at least show that he may have been at least partly wrong, both ethically and practically. On the ethical level, Machiavelli has no deontological answer but only a utilitarian one for Kant's insistence that it is wrong to treat other people merely as a means to an end and wrong to act in a way that we would not wish all others to act. And on the practical level, Aristotle's virtue ethics suggest that it may not be possible for a prince to do wrong only when it is useful.

That is, Aristotle's emphasis on habit may mean that it is impossible for a prince to do wrong only when it is useful. In the short run, the prince may do well by doing wrong. But what if wrongdoing becomes habitual for the prince so that he develops a vicious appetite? Such cruelty may earn the prince what Machiavelli warned was most dangerous to any ruler, the hatred of his subjects.

When the prince's subjects no longer respect but hate him, he is least secure. For even the most skillful prince will inevitably pass through periods of weakness. And when subjects sense weakness in a prince they hate, they will topple him for sure.

Leaders, in other words, are not in quite so black an ethical situation as Machiavelli thought. To say that the world is morally imperfect is not to say that it is perfectly immoral. It is only to say that there are no guarantees of success for anybody, good or bad. Bad guys do not automatically finish first. And to be a good guy is not necessarily to be a loser.

But a prince who wants to be honest needs all the competence and skill he can achieve. For Machiavelli was right that dishonesty is sometimes a competitive advantage. The prince who aspires to virtue therefore needs offsetting advantages such as exceptional competence to defeat unscrupulous enemies.

For the virtuous prince who wins there is a special moral danger of false pride in his integrity. It may turn him into an unwitting Machiavellian, which may have been what happened to George Bush in his Harken stock sale. Bush may have thought, whether consciously or unconsciously, that he had proven himself a moral leader in his good work for small shareholders in the rights offering, thereby reducing the moral caution that he needed when offered the chance to sell his stock.

So regarding the opening question of this chapter as to whether a better understanding of ethics would have helped Bush avoid the moral mistake of his stock sale, the admittedly unsatisfactory answer can only be that it might have. Bush needed moral caution. Understanding that moments of moral triumph such as he achieved in the rights offering are also moments of moral danger might but only might have given him the moral caution he needed.

For leaders to achieve the highest possible level of morality, they must paradoxically maintain the highest possible awareness that they are inevitably immoral. Executives blithely unaware of their immorality will deepen it. But good-willed leaders who understand that some degree of immorality is inherent in their positions will attempt to minimize it.

That is why the unrealistic moral optimism of today's leadership cult is so dangerous. It blinds executives to their moral dangers and may lead them into unwitting Machiavellianism. The possibility that that is what happened to Bush in his stock sale illustrates the danger of the lack of ethical understanding in the leadership cult.

Since it is impossible in this short book—and anyway would be terribly boring—to cover all possible examples of the lack of ethical understanding in the leadership cult, it must be dealt with representatively. A good example of such lack of ethical understanding is the bestselling book *Managing by Values* (1997). It is representative because many leadership gurus agree on using values to manage.

Given that leadership gurus are little accustomed to critical discussion, it may need emphasizing that I have no reason to think anything other than that the authors of *Managing by Values* are good people. Their book's mistake has been independently repeated by many others. The great influence of *Managing by Values* over the past decade—an eternity by the standard of management how-to manuals—is due to its expressing ideas that are common to many gurus.

Managing by Values makes its points via a thinly plotted, fictional account of a hitherto tyrannical boss who, by chance, encounters a sententious guru who emphasizes the importance of values in management. Needless to say, the tyrannical boss converts to managing by values. He aims to move his organization to the point where *"the real 'boss"* is not himself but, rather, *"the company's adopted values"*:[15]

Be ETHICAL
Be RESPONSIVE
Be PROFITABLE[16]

It would be nice if companies could "adopt" such values. But there is a problem in that values are not easily "adopted." Values are deeply rooted "normative beliefs" about "conduct (means) or an end-state (ends)."[17]

Values change, but usually not rapidly. It takes a radically new social situation, a personal crisis, or some other large challenge in our lives to change our values quickly. Otherwise, values change slowly, often unnoticeably.

Values do not change just because employees rank order 60 or 70 virtues from a list provided by a consultant and then "adopt" the top three.[18] Such exercises can be happy social experiences useful for getting to know co-workers. But if the resulting organizational "values" are genuine, it's not because the group "adopted" them but because, despite the naive process, the group managed to hit on values its members already shared.

Managing by Values pays lip service to the idea that to achieve self-knowledge "You have to dig deeper, to the level of your inner values."[19] But how do you dig? There's no advice offered, just the fictional example of a consultant who asks "By what values do you want your company to be known?"[20] It appears that the digging consists mainly in deciding what "values" to "adopt."

As religious seers and secular psychologists have long pointed out, it is no easy task to know what we value. Introspection is especially unreliable because the human heart so readily deceives itself. That's why "adopting" values is no more effective for organizations than New Year's resolutions are for individuals.

Self-examination has its best shot at success if it involves reflection on what one's behavior says about one's values. "By their fruits ye shall know them" is an ancient way of saying that our conduct indicates who we are and the things about which we really care. But objective self-examination focused on behavior does not enter the picture in *Managing by Values*.

Employees in the book's fictional company do not consider their conduct, let alone what that conduct says about what they really value. Instead, *Managing by Values* wrongly assumes that people automatically know their values. Worse, it assumes that people can acquire new and better values by just choosing to "adopt" them.

What is usually called managing by values is really just a deceptive way of managing by rules. The new "values" are not necessarily deeply held in employees' hearts and minds. Rather, they are new rules mistakenly called values. These new rules do at least have the additional advantage of having been adopted with employee input.

Managing by rules can be a good thing if it's done honestly. Then an employee doesn't have to "align" the heart and mind. He or she just has to learn the rules and do what they say without professing to embrace them as values.

Of course the whole objective of the leadership cult—and it can be a good goal—is to raise productivity by getting employees to invest their hearts and minds. But people can invest their hearts and minds in a company managed by rules. A leader managing by rules can demonstrate the integrity and competence that may win moral influence and convert subordinates into followers.

In fact, managing by rules is a better way of winning genuine moral influence than managing by values. If employees recognize—as they sometimes do—that managers who claim to be managing by values are really managing by rules, they may consider such managers deceptive and refuse to grant them moral influence. Managers who openly use rules to lead may well be more honest and competent and therefore achieve greater moral influence than those who use values to lead.

It's probably impossible actually to manage any large organization by values. It's not that values aren't important. But people already have their values and aren't likely to "adopt" new ones at the behest of a visiting management consultant. The whole idea of managing by values is a polite fiction.

If managing by values is a fiction, why does it often fatten the bottom line? The fictitiousness of managing by values can be key to its practical success. Managers who use values to lead run the risk of becoming unwitting Machiavellians. They may deceive not only others but also themselves.

Managing by values can give managers an illusion of being honest and ethical when they are anything but. When a CEO abolishes titles and calls everyone an "associate," he or she is not living "up to our Ethical value" but trying to create a fiction. The CEO may mean well in responding to "employee feedback on perceived hierarchical roles."[21] But egalitarianism is an impossible value in for-profit corporations. Some "associates" will always be more equal than others.

Pretensions of democracy sometimes serve the same function in management fads as pretensions of virtue in Machiavelli's recipe for princely success. Democratic and egalitarian sham can hide from followers and leaders alike the moral ambiguity inherent in a position of leadership. And just as Machiavelli said, deception sometimes gets results. The fiction of managing by values helps managers of conscience feel all right about working in a corporate hierarchy while professing the official, egalitarian values of their larger, democratic society.

Fictitious new "values" can be good for a company. The newly adopted values (rules, really) can get the CEO to try to move decision making closer to front-line employees, try to create an environment where employees feel safe in speaking their minds, and try to evaluate employees by performance rather than personality.[22] Like other management techniques that end up making similar common-sense recommendations, managing by values can be useful as a conjured carrot to get the corporate horse moving in the right direction.

Or is managing by values really a stick in disguise? The "alignment process" for closing "gaps" between an individual employee's performance and the company values may include an ombudsman, feedback tools, employee surveys, and so on.[23] And those can certainly be good things. But the goal of "alignment" with "values," which are supposedly the new "boss," is the same old, tragically inescapable, undemocratic, and necessary basis of corporate life—getting people in line.

The claim that values can be boss is really just one more variation on the great management myth that moral influence is mainly top down. But *Managing by Values* carries that fiction to its ultimate extent. The book prints an organization chart showing the CEO and the Board of Directors reporting to "Values" at the company's pinnacle.

It is true that we are all led by our values. But values printed at the top of an organization chart are unlikely to be the values that truly lead us. We are led by the complex jumble of good and bad things about which we really care. We don't always know what these values are, but are constantly discovering them through our behavior, sometimes to our honor and sometimes to our chagrin.

It can be morally more dangerous to bring others into line in the name of fictitious values than through naked power. "Managing by values" can make it easier for both leaders and followers to overestimate the leader's righteousness. After all, why is the manager the one doing the aligning if he or she is not more in tune with "values" than the person being aligned?

Such moral overestimation of a leader's values can be seen in a book of 2003, *The Leadership Genius of George W. Bush.* It was almost inevitable after 9/11, when Bush's approval ratings were in the stratosphere, that his example would be put to use perpetrating the leadership cult. The authors predictably tell us that Bush is an exemplary leader because "He is serious about his values."[24]

One of Bush's top values, the authors say, is "integrity." They base this judgment on Bush's 2000 campaign autobiography, *A Charge to Keep.* In short, Bush himself is the source of the authors' idea that he has shown the ability to make the right call when "integrity was at stake."[25]

Such research methods are all too typical of business leadership studies, which often rely heavily on interviews, autobiographies, and other first-person accounts by corporate heavy hitters. Such studies' conclusions obviously run the risk of being influenced by executives' self-serving interpretations of their actions. Such first-person accounts need to be balanced by research in objective sources such as the records of the SEC investigation of Bush's stock sale on which chapter 4 of this book is based.

Bush's Harken stock sale makes it clear that his relationship to integrity is more complicated than the authors of *The Leadership Genius of George W. Bush* believe. Bush has some integrity in him, but the authors of the book on Bush's leadership overestimate it. And they underestimate—or rather, say nothing at all—about the fact that Bush, like all the rest of us, has some bad values in him that sometimes make him fall short in integrity.

It would be wrong, however, to make Bush out as falling exceptionally short in integrity. That would be to risk deceiving ourselves. Anyone of us might have done no better if we had been confronted with the opportunity to make many thousands of dollars of extra profit in a morally mistaken stock sale. That does not mean that we should not hold others to account for their errors, but only that we ought to try to avoid self-righteousness while doing so.

Leaders like Bush deserve a lot more help on ethical issues than they usually get from the conventional wisdom on leadership. Instead of ethical understanding that would promote moral caution and self-examination, the leadership cult offers leaders ideas well suited for inflating their sense of themselves as moral paragons and desensitizing them to the real ethical challenges they face. Is it any wonder that CEOs are carted off to prison while protesting, sincerely, that they are not crooks but moral leaders?

Such failings of ethical understanding are practically as well as morally dangerous. Whether or not Machiavelli was right that the prince must sometimes deceive others, a ruler needs a clear mind himself. It is therefore risky for a prince to use values to lead. He may subvert values he means to support.

Chapter 6

Corporate Social Irresponsibility

So shattering was 9/11 that it is easy to forget that in the following 12 months the Bush administration also had to deal with the largest challenge to the moral standing of corporate capitalism since the Great Depression. Enron, WorldCom, Global Crossing, Qwest, Tyco, Adelphia, and a dozen lesser scandals, coming one on top of another, put in doubt the financial statements of every publicly held company in America. Bush tried to use values to lead the process of corporate reform. He succeeded only in making himself irrelevant to the historic transformation of government-business relations that took place during the second year of his presidency.

Enron stumbled toward collapse all through the months following September 11 and finally filed for bankruptcy in December 2001. In the following weeks the news media were filled with painful accounts of employees who had lost not just their jobs but their retirement funds which had been locked into Enron stock. The fear of millions of other corporate employees that a similar fate awaited them provoked political concern in the White House. In January 2002 Bush appointed two committees, both headed by his then Secretary of the Treasury, Paul O'Neill, to propose reforms in corporate pensions and corporate governance.

O'Neill pushed to raise the legal standards for CEO conduct. A former, highly successful CEO of the Alcoa Company, O'Neill believed the current laws were too easy on corporate chiefs. Only reckless or willful misrepresentations of their companies' financial statements could get executives in legal trouble. Senior managers at Enron and many other scandal-ridden firms tried to shield themselves behind that standard.

They had not known what was going on, they said, and therefore had not recklessly misled investors.

O'Neill, supported by Federal Reserve Chairman Alan Greenspan, proposed to change the legal standard from reckless to *negligent* misrepresentation. That would make it harder for CEOs to plead ignorance. The question would be whether they had carefully tried to make sure that they knew the truth and had tried to speak it to investors. CEOs who negligently misrepresented the facts would be just as guilty as if they had been reckless or fraudulent.

O'Neill believed that enactment of his negligence standard would frighten CEOs into action. Staring at a legal abyss if guilty of carelessness, CEOs would hold accountants and auditors to a high standard of performance. Investors would finally be able to believe the financial statements of companies in which they owned shares.

CEOs were scared for sure by what they saw as O'Neill's unreasonable proposal. After he presented his ideas to a hostile business audience, one executive replied that he would "resign rather than be expected to know everything that's going on in my company … I simply can't be held responsible for what all of those people do."[1]

Actually, a legal standard of negligence would not require a CEO to know everything going on. It would just require him or her to try find out. A CEO who carefully tried to find out what was going on but was still deceived by criminal subordinates would not have been liable under O'Neill's negligence standard.

The argument between O'Neill and the CEOs was not really about legal standards but about the cult of moral leadership and its disdain for managing. The CEO who said he couldn't be responsible for his subordinates' actions was really saying that his job was to lead rather than to manage his company. He was willing to use moral influence, but he was not ready to earn moral influence through hands-on management.

Concerned CEOs were soon lobbying the White House as to the unreasonableness of the Treasury Secretary's proposal. The corporate chiefs dreamed up bogeymen such as a nightmarish wave of litigation if O'Neill's plan was enacted. But O'Neill planned to bar civil lawsuits and to leave enforcement of the negligence standard up to the government alone.

CEOs also said that O'Neill's proposal was overkill. Companies with questionable accounting were already being punished with massive sell-offs of their stock. That showed, according to the corporate chiefs, that the free market was correcting itself. The fact that innocent investors were suffering massive losses while the market went about correcting corporate fraud did not concern the CEOs.

So it came down to a frightened part of Bush's political base, corporate CEOs, versus his Treasury Secretary. The CEOs wanted business as usual. O'Neill wanted responsible CEOs, an idea consistent with the Bush administration's call for a new era of personal responsibility.

But were CEOs to be made responsible by force of law or by values? Bush opted to use values rather than legislation to lead the way toward corporate reform. Abandoning O'Neill's proposal to change the legal standard from recklessness to negligence, Bush—probably seeing himself as one moral leader speaking to others—called on CEOs to fulfill their responsibilities to investors, employees, and the public in general.

Part of Bush's decision was practical politics. His governing strategy was far from centrist. Rather, he aimed to energize his conservative base, which included CEOs.

But after 9/11 Bush's approval ratings were running above 80 percent. It would have required little political courage to take on the CEOs. The corporate chiefs were vastly outnumbered by citizens, employees, and investors who wanted action.

With broad public support for corporate reform, Bush could have rallied a coalition of Republicans and Democrats to support a proposal like O'Neill's. Since Democrats were ready for far stronger measures, Bush might therefore have brought them along on O'Neill's proposal. And because O'Neill's idea would not have directly interfered in companies' internal operations, it was consistent with conservative Republicans' goal of maximizing responsibility rather than regulation.

By abandoning O'Neill's proposal, Bush lost a great opportunity to exercise moral leadership. A measure such as O'Neill's was needed, supportable by Democrats, and consistent with conservative Republicans' individualist ideology. Politicians rarely find so many ducks lined up before they even begin to hunt. Bush failed to seize the opportunity.

By missing this chance at moral leadership, Bush also made a major strategic error that defeated his goal of minimal regulatory interference in business operations. His failure to act left a leadership vacuum that eventually led to the Sarbanes-Oxley Act (SOX), the sort of intense government regulation loathed by both Bush and many corporate chiefs. Today, angry CEOs say that the high cost of conforming to SOX impairs their ability to compete globally.

In the absence of presidential leadership, the push for reform came from employees, investors, and the public in general. Ordinary citizens did not believe that Bush's appeal to CEOs' good values would do the job. An angry public was about to force major regulatory change on corporate America.

In short, Bush and the CEOs got a taste of the democratic principle that morality can be bottom-up instead of top-down. By siding with the CEOs, Bush disengaged, though he probably did not know it, from the process of corporate reform in 2002. Congress eventually took the lead in responding to public outrage while the president did little except to utter moral pieties.

The CEOs would actually have been better off if they had had a president less committed to leading with values and more willing to challenge them with power. But Bush seems to have really believed that CEOs were moral leaders to whose values he could successfully appeal. Many of them were of course honest to a large degree. Still, Bush overestimated their integrity on the whole. He clung for months to the idea that corporate fraud was a matter of a "few bad apples."[2]

What was really wrong with corporate ethics was symbolized not just by a few CEOs in handcuffs, but by the many CEOs, and many other executives as well, who grew wealthy from off-the-books stock options. Corporations' refusal to expense the stock options that they granted to company officers as incentive compensation became widely known at the same time that Enron and other corporate chimeras were collapsing into dust. Off-the-books options had made the earnings statements of many companies unreliable in a way not too dissimilar to Enron's. The difference was that, instead of booking phony revenue, companies failed to book real expenses.

When companies granted stock options to their officers, they did not enter the options on the books as an expense. Years later, when an executive exercised the option to buy stock at some earlier, lower price, the company would either issue stock from its treasury, diluting shareholder value, or else buy shares in the market, raising current costs. Investors who wanted to know the cost of employee stock options could only try to find out by doing their own calculations on the basis of figures that were required to be disclosed in companies' financial reports but which were not required to be included in the process of computing those reports' statements of earnings and losses.

Many CEOs and other corporate officials had difficulty understanding the moral issue. The usual reason for exercising an option is that a company has done well, raising the price of the stock and benefiting all shareholders. So what was the harm with using options to reward management for a job well done? The fact that often got left out of the discussion was that corporate officials might be tempted to help themselves to piles of lucre from the company treasury not by doing their jobs well but by short-term accounting gimmicks that temporarily inflated earnings, pushed up the stock price, and put their options above water.

A few capitalist luminaries like Warren Buffett pointed out that it wasn't a question of rewarding deserving executives. It was a question of giving them honest incentives for honest management. And investors deserved accurate information as to how much money their companies were making and how much they were paying their companies' managers.

Congress had attempted to reform corporate accounting for stock options during the 1990s. But corporate management easily fended off those reform efforts. CEOs claimed that options were a recruiting tool that brought on board skilled managers who enhanced American competitiveness.

In the wake of Enron, the integrity of corporate accounting became a subject of much wider interest than was customary. At annual meetings, shareholders were beginning to present resolutions demanding reform on options. Bush, afraid of angering the CEOs in his political base, offered no comment on stock options in early 2002 when leadership on the issue was most needed.

Meanwhile, rumors swirled about Global Crossing and Qwest. Each had to announce in early 2002 that it was a subject of an SEC investigation. And the Justice Department prepared to indict Arthur Andersen, Enron's auditor, for impeding the SEC investigation of that company. The travails of all three companies would fill the media till late spring. Public anger would only grow.

Anger had already surged in the lower ranks of corporate America. Photographs of CEOs in handcuffs encouraged employees to tip off the SEC as to the dirt at their own companies. Picking up the phone and spilling the beans on their putative moral leaders, corporate employees forced the SEC to open triple its usual number of investigations during early 2002. Even Harvey Pitt, Bush's SEC chairman, notoriously insensitive to auditors' conflicts of interest, requested money for additional investigators. The White House coolly said he would "have to make his case."[3]

Bush gave no appearance of realizing that a crisis of historic proportions was underway. He warned that the most important thing was to avoid overzealous legislation that would "encourage frivolous lawsuits."[4] In early March he offered a tepid ten-point plan for corporate reform.

Bush called for CEOs to sign their companies' financial statements but, as penalties for misrepresentation, suggested only forfeiture of salaries and bonuses. He sensibly wanted to bar accounting firms from conflicts of interest between their consulting and auditing businesses. For the rest, Bush would tweak some SEC regulations. CEOs, thanking their lucky stars for their friend in the White House, had no more idea than Bush that he had made himself irrelevant by offering so weak a reform plan.

A similar, do-little spirit dominated the House of Representatives. The Financial Services Committee, chaired by Republican Michael Oxley, sent a reform bill to the floor in mid-April. The House quickly passed Oxley's measure, which resembled Bush's plan in specifics and in tepidness. Bush praised the bill and urged the Senate to enact it.

But the Senate, controlled by Democrats, was working on a far tougher bill. Paul Sarbanes, chairman of the Banking Committee, aimed to subject corporate management to an unprecedented level of regulation. CEOs would not only have to sign corporate financial statements, they would be required to include in a company's annual report an assessment of its internal control and accounting processes.

Unlike Bush, Sarbanes would not settle for appealing to CEOs' values while only requiring them to vouch for the accuracy of their financial reporting. He aimed to force them to manage their accounting and control functions. Hands-on management, not values and vouching, would make for accurate financial statements.

Sarbanes also proposed to create a Public Company Accounting Oversight Board within the SEC. It would work in collaboration with the Financial Accounting Standards Board (FASB). FASB, funded by the accounting industry, was the nongovernmental organization to which the SEC had long ceded its regulatory power over accounting.

FASB had a record of integrity but too little clout. It had tried, for example, to raise the issue of off-the-books options in the past but had given in to corporate opposition. The new Public Company Accounting Oversight Board proposed by Sarbanes would operate from within the SEC, would bolster the spirit of integrity at FASB, and would have a majority of members from outside the accounting profession. Obviously, off-the-books stock options were doomed if the Sarbanes bill passed.

The corporate establishment was little concerned about Sarbanes' bill, which was considered too radical to take seriously. Some Democrats agreed, believing that the bill's only use would be the chance to blame Republicans for killing it. The Bush administration, probably fearing just such repercussions, kept a low profile. Quietly, the White House put out the word that there was, in one reporter's summary, no need for "far-reaching legislation and regulation proposed largely by the Democrats."[5]

But Sarbanes was a skillful parliamentarian. Some minor concessions to Republicans—plus an assist from the conviction of Arthur Andersen a few days earlier—enabled Sarbanes to get his bill through the Senate Banking Committee in mid-June with a 17–4 vote. The lopsided vote indicated that Sarbanes' proposal went to the Senate floor not as a strictly Democratic bill, as the White House was saying, but with considerable Republican support.

And while Sarbanes' bill was coming to life, a new wave of corporate scandals was filling the media. SEC investigations of Adelphia, Tyco, and WorldCom were beginning to reveal some of the most corrupt and colorful CEO excesses yet. There seemed to be no end to corporate venality. Doubts began to be voiced as to the quality of earnings at well-established giants like General Electric.

Adding to the loss of public confidence in the business system was the unabashed arrogance of the newly discredited CEOs. Enron's Jeff Skilling, testifying to a congressional committee in February, had been a model of superciliousness while blaming his subordinates for the company's corruption. Bernie Ebbers of WorldCom came across as a prayerful hypocrite and self-righteous bully. When the Arthur Andersen accounting firm was convicted in June, its unrepentant leaders blamed the government for an unjust prosecution.

Investors were voting with their feet or, rather, their sell orders. The Dow Jones Industrial Average, having lost 6 percent in 2000 and 7 percent in 2001, fell another 8 percent for the first six months of 2002, the worst first half year in three decades. Foreign capital was leaving the stock market, indicating that the U.S. was losing its reputation as the world's safest country in which to invest. Polls showed that even though the economy was growing, a majority of Americans thought it was in recession, an opinion that could spell bad news for Republicans in the midterm election coming up in November 2002.

In the last week of June, the SEC required WorldCom to restate its earnings for 2001 and the first quarter of 2002, revealing that bogus accounting had inflated its profits by $3.8 billion in that period. A few days later WorldCom had to take another $1 billion off its profits for 1999 and 2000. The company, soon in default on its obligations, was obviously headed for a colossal collapse.

Corporate scandals and what the president was doing about them began to dominate the daily White House press briefings. Bush scheduled a trip to New York on July 9 to speak on corporate reform. But in the first week of July, the media dug up the old Harken dirt and Bush's involvement in it.

So on July 8, the day before Bush was going to speak on integrity to the New York moneymen, he had to hold a hastily arranged press conference to defend his Harken conduct. Reporters did not have the information on the inadequacy of the SEC investigation of Bush that is provided in chapter 4 of this book. They therefore left unchallenged Bush's insistence that the SEC had cleared him of wrongdoing in his insider sale.

But on other Harken issues, Bush came off badly. Reporters asked about the SEC's forcing Harken to restate its 1989 earnings while he was on the company's audit committee. Bush, the self-proclaimed opponent of everything gray, said that "sometimes things aren't exactly black and white when it comes to accounting." Queried as to why he had violated SEC rules by late reporting of his Harken stock sale, he told reporters, "I still haven't figured it out completely."[6] It wasn't clear that the president had done much better at his press conference than had WorldCom executives who appeared before Congress on the same day and declined to answer lest they incriminate themselves.

Yet Bush still believed that he could address the corporate crisis through moral leadership. The day after his inept press conference, he traveled to New York to deliver a rhetorically rousing but substantively empty speech. Instead of taking action to end off-the-books options, Bush called for voluntary disclosure: "I challenge every CEO in America to describe in the company's annual report prominently and in plain English the details of his or her compensation package."[7] One suspects that the CEOs who most needed to put that one on their to-do lists were the ones who did not.

Bush announced that he would ask Congress to double the prison terms for some white collar crimes and to appropriate more money for SEC enforcement efforts. And he was ordering the Justice Department to create a task force on corporate fraud, a "financial crimes SWAT team."[8] But he followed those token tough gestures by making it clear that he was sticking with his and Oxley's tepid reform legislation.

More experienced in corporate politesse than any previous president, Bush ended his New York speech by implying that the most powerful people in his audience were also the most moral: "Leaders in this room help give the free enterprise system an ethical compass. And the nation respects you for that. We need that influence now more than ever."[9] The CEOs, sharing Bush's wishful hope that moral leadership would suffice to restore confidence in corporate America, praised his moderation.

Investors were having none of it and expressed their lack of confidence in the corporate world's supposed moral leaders by sending the market tumbling. The Dow, down by 104 points on the day of Bush's lame defense of his Harken conduct, lost another 179 points the next day when he spoke in New York. The day after that, the Dow fell yet another 283 points, putting it 40 percent beneath where it had opened in January 2000.

Congressional Republicans were running scared. It was fine for Bush, with over two years left in his term, to pander to CEOs. But a third of Senators and every member of the House were up for re-election in November 2002. Voter anger was running high.

Republicans in Congress therefore got religion on corporate reform. Their born-again faith in government regulation solidified on July 15 when Bush, speaking at the University of Alabama, tried to reassure jittery investors: "The economy is coming back.... That is the fact."[10] An hour later the Dow was down 440 points. Opportunistic buying restored most of the loss by the end of the day. But sad sacks in the business media rightly opined that the bear market's bottom was nowhere in sight.

That same day, July 15, the Sarbanes bill was rushed to a Senate vote amid a sense of emergency. On the day in which Bush had tried to reassure the stock market only to have it go off a cliff, the Senate approved Sarbanes' bill 97–0. The legislation which only a few weeks earlier seemed too radical to take seriously now passed on a unanimous vote! The sudden appeal of the Sarbanes bill lay in the fact that it alone proposed the real change that angry voters were demanding.

The conservative Oxley measure and the radical Sarbanes bill would now go for reconciliation to a House-Senate conference committee, the traditional slaughtering ground for reform legislation. Conservative Republicans, fearful of public opinion, had voted for the Sarbanes bill in the Senate. Now they hoped to water it down in conference. CEOs and other corporate statesmen had their lobbyists ready to make reason prevail behind closed doors.

But with voters baying for justice, most congressional Republicans saw the danger as doing too little, not too much. By now even the conservative Oxley was a draconian reformer. Astonishingly, he pronounced his bill "very similar" to Sarbanes'.[11]

Dennis Hastert, the conservative Republican House Speaker, converted to corporate reform and found the Senate bill acceptable. Some House members even suggested dropping the Oxley bill, skipping the conference committee, and just enacting the Sarbanes bill in the form that it had been sent to them by the Senate. Bush, jumping on the caboose before the train left without him, signaled that he would sign whatever corporate reform legislation Congress sent him.[12]

If the conference committee members felt their reformist resolve weakening when they met from July 22 to 24, they just had to look at the headlines. The story broke that Citigroup and J. P. Morgan Chase had been complicit in the burnishing of Enron's financial statements. Halliburton, the multinational of which Vice President Cheney had been CEO, came under investigation for its accounting practices.

So the conference committee, instead of weakening the Sarbanes bill, stiffened it. Oxley got some of the prison sentences lengthened. And he shortened the reporting time for insider trading. At the conclusion of the conference, Sarbanes graciously suggested naming his bill the Sarbanes-Oxley Act. So the conservative Oxley who had fought the legislation until ten days earlier became forever associated with the largest change in government regulation of business since the Great Depression.

Bush tried to make the best of his defeat by pretending it was a victory. Enactment of Sarbanes-Oxley, according to his press secretary, marked "a day of action and accomplishment in the president's fight against corporate corruption."[13] At the signing ceremony on July 30, Bush said that the act embraced the core principles of his reform plan, neglecting to add that it went ten miles further and in the opposite direction.

Bush rightly declared Sarbanes-Oxley "the most far-reaching reform of American business practices since the time of Franklin Delano Roosevelt."[14] He did not add, as Sarbanes frankly admitted, that the act was modeled on Roosevelt-style New Deal legislation. SOX set up an intense regulatory regime, thwarting Bush's preference for appealing to CEOs as moral leaders rather than subjecting them to government control.

SOX forced corporate America to spend billions of dollars building parallel processes to control and account for their control and accounting functions. The high tech industry profited thanks to all the new computers needed to implement SOX. The 27,000 Arthur Andersen employees who had lost their jobs when a court put their company out of business found themselves in a vastly expanded market for pixel pushers. Business schools happily set to work training the legions of new accountants required to implement SOX.

The SOX requirement to assess accounting and control amounted to a regressive tax on small, entrepreneurial companies. To implement SOX cost small firms less, but not proportionately less. So the companies that could least afford it and that created most of the new jobs in America had, in relative terms, the heaviest new load to carry.

As the new law came into effect in 2004, word spread that small companies were avoiding Sarbanes-Oxley by not going public, thereby denying themselves access to the capital that they needed to grow. Start-ups began obtaining corporate charters overseas to avoid SOX. Many small companies, perhaps 60 percent of all publicly held companies in the United States, simply broke the law and failed to comply with SOX.[15]

So began the process of reforming Sarbanes-Oxley and making it manageable for small companies. For the large firms who are obeying it, SOX creates plenty of new costs. And SOX still has many loopholes, the closing or expansion of which will fuel future legislative battles and give employment to lobbyists.

In effect, the American people, acting through Congress, finally said to corporate CEOs, "Enough leading. Start managing. And we're going to have the government show you how to do it. Find out what's going on in your companies, get control of it, and tell us the truth."

Final responsibility for this deep governmental involvement in the internal operations of business lies not just with corporate CEOs and George Bush but also with the leadership cult. Many of the CEOs who profited from off-the-books options believed themselves to be moral leaders. But they could not see the moral importance of giving investors information as good as possible on earnings and expenses. Only a change in the law, not Bush's appeal to CEOs as moral leaders, got the business executives in line. After SOX, FASB finally required companies to expense employee stock options.

If the resulting transparency and honesty give investors a chance to make better decisions on where capital can best be used, the economic benefit of SOX may—or may not—be worth the cost. All that is certain is that the CEOs who were pleased when Bush abandoned O'Neill's proposal now have a complicated and costly new law to obey. If given a second chance, the CEOs would surely jump at the chance to support O'Neill's simple change of their legal liability from recklessness to negligence.

O'Neill's proposal, like SOX, would have forced CEOs to pay less attention to leading and more to managing. But it would have left executives far more freedom in deciding how to manage. Under a friendly president who tried to lead them by values, CEOs ended up being less free and more highly managed themselves than they would ever have thought possible.

The conventional wisdom on leadership and values makes it difficult to learn from mistakes. To use values to lead is, by definition, to be in the right. Losing a fight such as Bush lost over corporate reform can therefore easily be interpreted as a reflection on the wrongness of one's opponents rather than on the idea of using values to lead.

Bush kept on using values to lead in the area of government and corporate relations. In 2003 he used the value of fairness to call for elimination of "double taxation of dividends." In his State of the Union address that year, Bush said, "It's fair to tax a company's profits. It is not fair to again tax the shareholder on the same profits." He asked Congress to end "unfair double taxation" by making dividends tax free.

Bush ignored the fact that a corporation is a separate person in the eyes of the law. It is not double taxation to tax two different persons. And it doesn't matter that the same money is taxed twice. The $20 bill with which I buy my haircut is taxed twice, once when I earn it and again when my barber earns it. No one calls this double taxation because everyone recognizes that the barber and I are separate people. Similarly, a corporation and a shareholder are separate people in the eyes of the law, and it is not unfair to tax them both.

Investors derive huge advantages such as limited liability from the corporation's separate personhood. But many shareholders were understandably happy with Bush's specious argument that when a company paid its own income tax it also paid theirs. Congress, though it did not abolish the dividend tax, reduced it far below the marginal tax rate of ordinary middle-class families.

Bush probably sincerely believes that a low tax on dividends is sound economic policy. And he may be right. But he was wrong to argue for taxing dividends at a lower rate than other income on grounds of fairness.

That it is possible to get such obviously unfair tax policy enacted in the name of fairness is just one more example of how morally ambiguous the world, and especially its leaders, can be. Misleading arguments on the basis of values such as "fairness" will probably always be a part of leadership. But though such false arguments are inevitable, they should be answered.

False arguments on the basis of values are sometimes defeated. Such was the case on Bush's largest domestic initiative following his 2004 re-election, his drive to "reform" Social Security. Actually he aimed to replace the value Americans place on Social Security with the values of individualism and private property.

Bush had scarcely mentioned Social Security during his campaign for re-election, which he won by a thin margin. But after the election he claimed he had earned the "political capital" to replace the country's most highly valued social program by investing employees' payroll taxes in individual stock market accounts. He aimed to fulfill his vision of an "ownership society" built on the values of individualism and private property.

He missed the fact that while Americans overwhelmingly believe in individualism and private property, they also have other values. Social Security's popularity reflects people's commitment to values such as security and sharing. Any politician setting out to reform Social Security will succeed only by respecting the values on which so popular a program is based.

Maybe the stock market is a good place to invest the Social Security trust fund. But to propose to invest that money via individual accounts is to attack the value of *Social* Security. Any successful change of Social Security will not be of the every-ship-on-its-own-bottom variety.

Bush's various attempts to use values to lead have put him in the wrong on the corporate issues facing his administration. When reform was possible and justified, as on corporate governance, he saw no need for forceful action, but relied on moral leadership—the failure of which led to stiff regulation he opposed. He wrongly invoked the value of fairness to unfairly reduce taxes on corporate dividends. And he tried to divert Social Security payroll taxes into the corporate economy under a plan disingenuously labeled "reform" when it actually amounted to abolition of Social Security.

Bush's moral failures as a CEO-style leader using values to manage suggest how mistaken are the all-too-common attempts to substitute moral leadership for ethical understanding, situational knowledge, and professional competence. Genuinely moral leadership is a tough and, at best, only partially achievable challenge. The difficulty of moral leadership ought to make CEOs and indeed all corporate managers doubly skeptical that they can exercise spiritual leadership at work.

Chapter 7

Spirituality at Work

On Palm Sunday 2002 President Bush could not attend church. He was in the air, returning from an overseas trip. So his staff organized a worship service on Air Force One. National Security Advisor Condoleezza Rice led the hymns, and Presidential Counselor Karen Hughes offered a homily.

Bush later said that he felt "the presence of God" on the plane: "to be able to worship with people with whom you work in a unique spot is a special moment."[1] He was surely right. Only the most hardened cynic could deny that spiritual connectedness at work is personally precious and organizationally useful.

"Spirituality at work" is a hot topic among leadership gurus and management professors these days. Bush, long out of the corporate world and longer still out of business school, may not even know about the movement for spirituality at work. But he has a natural affinity for this trendy management fad.

The movement for workplace spirituality is the logical conclusion of the leadership cult. Proponents admit that "spiritual leadership" is a "natural consequence" of the "rise of values-based transformational leadership ideas."[2] It is scarcely surprising that Bush, who so often uses values to lead, has also tried to put spirituality to work.

According to the leadership cult, a top job is a mark of moral elevation. From there it is only a small step to the conclusion that good leaders must have spiritual, even holy qualities. Imagine what pinnacles these paragons can ascend by using not just values but spirituality to lead!

Thanks to George Bush, a national experiment is underway in leading by spirituality. His program of Faith-Based Initiatives surely owes much to his personal encounters with demon rum and religious redemption. But the program probably also owes more of its origins than has been noticed to Bush's business education, business experience, and his almost lifelong exposure to the leadership cult.

As opposed to the U.S. Constitution's separation of church and state, management seers often join Christianity and corporation. Leadership gurus teach a model of personal and organizational transformation that is subtly patterned on Pauline conversion. The gurus often use the popular phrase for religious converts—"twice born"—to describe the way in which leaders are created.

Explicitly evangelical content is usually expurgated from management doctrine in order to accommodate it to a multifaith workforce. But the notion that leaders can be created by undergoing a redeeming rebirth of the psyche remains intact. Many business leaders have been taught an implicitly Christian notion of leaders' personalities that gives additional allure to the spirituality-at-work fad.

But it is spiritually dangerous to aim at a spiritual renaissance in a corporate context. Just as managing by values subverts rather than supports values, managing by spirituality can subvert spirituality at work. Business leaders aiming at spiritual renewal in the workplace may mistake vainglory for inner purity.

Leaving aside the interesting question of whether CEOs enjoy divine grace in greater or lesser proportion than the rest of us, it is safe to say that in a psychological sense not many corporate honchos are twice born. Most CEOs are solid personalities. They have little if any clue as to the pain involved in having one's identity truly smelted in some crisis of the spirit.

Of course CEOs often face challenges that test their personalities. But they meet those challenges by holding their selves intact, not by a shattering and rebuilding of their personalities. To describe CEOs' mostly fortunate lives as "twice born" runs the risk of encouraging them to overestimate their supposedly pain-wrought piety.

George Bush's swearing off alcohol is an example of the kind of personal experience that a CEO influenced by the leadership cult can misinterpret as evidence of a "twice born" qualification for leadership. Pundits have observed that Bush's overcoming a drinking problem helps "cast his persona in the mold that American voters most love: the Comeback Kid or the Underdog." To have triumphed over alcohol relieves him of the charge of having had, as a Bush, an easy, unchallenged life: "For the sake of the narrative of the American Dream, George W. needed to be the Prodigal Son."[3]

But it is not clear that Bush was ever more than an excessive social drinker who could get obnoxious at a party. There are no reports of his ever having been drunk at work. And he has said himself that he was never addicted to alcohol.

Bush's cold turkey embrace of sobriety at the age of 40 was an act of personal responsibility duplicated every day by other ex-drinkers, ex-smokers, and ex-drug abusers who claim no special virtue on account of it. It is impossible to know whether Bush gives himself excessive moral credit for his teetotalling. But there is greater than normal danger of doing so in any executive who subscribes to the leadership cult with its encouragement of self-congratulation.

Writers on spiritual leadership sometimes run the risk of playing to corporate managers' vanity by urging them to become shepherds. Fitness for leadership is supposedly indicated by an executive's "degree of comfort ... in providing spiritual care. As leaders commit to care of the whole person, they must include spiritual care into their practice."[4]

Such ideas can be the first step not toward spiritual liberation but toward spiritual oppression at work. Even before the movement for spirituality at work, there were managers interested in the "whole person," thanks to the leadership cult. Confident in their ability to manage not just workplace performance but employees' whole lives, they often hurt those they arrogantly thought they could help.

Bush has personally provided a good example of how a manager trying to foster spirituality at work can end up abusing subordinates' religious freedom. Not long after taking office in 2001, he began opening cabinet meetings with prayer. The report by one of Bush's cabinet members that his praying "had put off many cabinet secretaries when he started the practice in the first days of the administration"[5] suggests that he did not first get their consent.

The president should have told the cabinet members before they took their jobs that praying with him would be one of their duties. Or if Bush got the idea after appointing his cabinet, he should at minimum have discussed it with them. But he appears to have just dropped the job of praying with him on his subordinates.

If indeed that is the way it was, it probably seemed like moral and spiritual leadership to Bush. But it was really both a practical mistake and an abuse of power. He not only "put off" some of his subordinates but forfeited his right to the spiritual influence he sought to use as a leader.

For the president to open cabinet meetings with prayer without asking subordinates' permission violates the democratic principle that the conscience is not to be compelled. Cabinet members who did not want to pray with Bush could only keep silent or else confront and possibly alienate their boss. The cabinet members whose consciences rebelled seem to have felt compelled to keep their misgivings to themselves.

George Bush is scarcely the only boss to have sinned against democracy by imposing prayer on subordinates. The corporate criminal Bernie Ebbers, in his halcyon days as CEO of WorldCom, led employees in entreating divine favor. Only God can judge the spirit in which Ebbers prayed, but it was hard for mere mortals to detect much religious humility in his petitions to the Almighty. Regardless, he was abusing his power.

Political indoctrination under cover of spiritual leadership is another abuse of power that happens all too often in the workplace. The main violators are bosses who want to do more than just express their religious views to subordinates. They also want to explain the political implication of those views for issues such as abortion and gay rights.

These corporate Savonarolas justify themselves—or so I have been told by employees subjected to their tyranny—with the idea that in a seamless universe employees need to know their leaders. Misguided by the leadership cult, such executives believe they would fail in their responsibility as moral leaders if they did *not* discuss their religious views with employees. And while it is surely a tiny minority, some corporate executives follow Bush still more closely by forcing prayer on subordinates.

Bush is right that good leadership can spiritually transform people and organizations. But forcing prayer on subordinates is poor leadership. Employees, sensitive both to the boss's power and to the satisfaction he or she gets from the self-designated role of spiritual leader, may give the appearance of voluntarily joining in. But as with some of Bush's cabinet members, subordinates may actually resent the prayer.

Corporate executives aspiring to spiritual leadership should recognize that their organizational power is a spiritual hindrance. Possessing mundane power, they have their best shot at promoting spirituality by not promoting it. By refusing to adopt any explicit program for spirituality at work, managers can guard themselves against the temptation to try to propagate their faith and thereby spiritually deaden the workplace.

The best understanding of the right relation of spirituality and the workplace came from the great management theorist Mary Parker Follett (1869–1933). She argued that human identity is a series of related experiences and ideas. In other words, we are contained in spirit rather than spirit being in us.

The fact that our identities are essentially spiritual rather than physical explains, according to Follett, why working with other people can be so satisfying. When we communicate with others at work, we join our spirits with theirs. A part of our selves has literally joined others in a larger spirit.

By joining spiritually with others we rightly feel that we have become bigger souls, more connected and less alien to the world around us than previously. As the greatest philosopher of Follett's era said, we are not contained in our bodies, not "shut up in a box of flesh and blood."[6] Whether at work or in other parts of our lives, it is possible to participate in a being larger than ourselves.

Follett's idea also explains why working with others can be so frustrating. When we try but fail to reach a state of shared ideas, we have failed to achieve larger spirituality and can end up feeling isolated not just from co-workers but from whatever community of spirits may be possible in this world. Leaders owe it to followers, and vice versa, to try to foster the communication and cooperation that can enlarge each other's spirits.

That's why it's wrong for a boss to propagate religion among employees. To have doctrines dropped on them by a person of power will give many employees the feeling not of spiritual growth but of spiritual shrinking. Such an experience of smallness in the face of imposed beliefs is the essence of life under tyranny.

The democratic principle is that the conscience should not be compelled. That principle underlies separation of church and state. It is equally good for church and corporation.

Instead of managing *by* spirituality, it is better to manage *for* spirituality. A leader can work for spirituality by doing his or her best to help employees communicate and cooperate in a way that joins and enlarges their spirits. A leader who creates such a work environment does not have to say the word "spirituality"—much less discuss religious beliefs—to have a spiritual effect.

Conversely, the leader who wears his or her spirituality on the sleeve and self-consciously tries to use it as a management tool is less likely to have any genuinely spiritual influence. Some employees, rather than working with others in a spirit-enlarging fashion, will protect their personal autonomy by putting up spiritual walls. And the manager who tried to use spirituality as a management tool will have debased it by subordinating spirituality to what should have been a lesser purpose.

Maybe it's all right, as is increasingly common, to have a company chaplain. A chaplain is more likely than a manager to be respectful of diverse faiths and the rights of atheists when leading, say, a memorial gathering for a deceased colleague. A chaplain is more likely to understand the importance of resisting the temptation to corrupt the spirituality in such an occasion by trying to use it for the company's benefit.

But some clerical advocates of workplace spirituality recommend going much further than hiring a company chaplain. They want managers to encourage or at least facilitate open expression of religion at work. They want employees to be free to express their spirituality in explicitly religious rituals and symbols.

Proponents of open religious expression at work are often deeply sensitive to issues of diversity. They want to promote not managerial theocracy but "respectful pluralism" in the workplace.[7] The trouble is that managers would have to decide, for example, whether it is respectful or disrespectful to Jews, Hindus, Muslims, atheists and others for a Christian employee to hang a poster by her desk that says "Jesus Saves."

Obviously, managers who encourage such workplace religious expression are likely to create division, not unifying spirituality. Even the best-willed managers may favor—or be perceived as favoring—their own faiths. What seems like respectful religious expression to a manager can feel, to subordinates, like conversion by clout.

Advocates of religion at work try to present themselves as friends of freedom by pointing out that people "bring the basic aspects of their identity to the workplace."[8] By encouraging expression of religious identity at work, corporate leaders can evidently become human liberators. Jefferson, Bolivar, and Mazzini, make way for CEOs!

The idea that religion should be expressed in the workplace because employees bring their religious identities to work is as nonsensical as some other management theories. Employers do not encourage workplace expression of sexuality even though it is a "basic aspect" of human identity that employees cannot leave at home. Too often, it is not an honest desire for human liberation but, rather, a manipulative desire to motivate the workforce that is the fundamental driver of the movement for spirituality at work.

Advocates of religious expression at work are right that people carry their faith with them wherever they go. But they are mistaken as to the meaning of that fact. The omnipresence of faith means that a good way for corporations to shut spirituality out of the workplace is to try to import religion into it.

Conferences on workplace spirituality usually feature well-known business leaders but not, to my knowledge, front-line employees. No doubt some employees are grateful for opportunities for religious expression at work. But many others—possibly the great majority— prefer to reserve religious expression for the home and for worship places where participants have come freely for that express purpose.

It is the spirituality-at-work movement that wrongly treats spirituality as if it had not always been in the workplace. From that mistaken starting point it seems obvious that spirituality should be brought to work from church, temple, or mosque. The result will of course be sectarian division more likely to shrink than enlarge employees' souls.

So the best practice is to manage not *by* spirituality but *for* it. Instead of using spirituality to get good work, managers can use good work to join employees into larger spirits. Running the organization honestly and competently so as to enable people to work well together is the best way to help employees find whatever spiritual transcendence is possible in corporate life.

The corporate world can learn how to make employees' spirits soar by studying the example of the first amendment to the Constitution of the United States. It prohibits Congress from making any law "respecting an establishment of religion," a prohibition that accounts for the extraordinary thriving of religion in America. In many countries with government-supported religious establishments, a much smaller percentage of the people identify themselves as believers than in the United States. A good strategy to weaken religion is to give it official support.

Unfortunately, the wrong teacher is at the head of the class. Instead of management gurus learning from the Constitution, the government has been adopting a religious policy consistent with the leadership cult. Bush's program of Faith-Based Initiatives has won votes from religious fundamentalists by giving them access to the federal Treasury, but it is most likely a defeat for the religious spirit in America.

Bush's program of government funding for Faith-Based Initiatives is a sort of national program for spirituality at work. The CEO—i.e., Bush—is using spirituality to accomplish his organization's—i.e., the nation's—goal of more effective social service programs. Management fads seldom get tested on so large a scale.

The germ of Faith-Based Initiatives came from a 1993 meeting between Bush and Marvin Olasky, a professor at the University of Texas and author of *The Tragedy of American Compassion* (1992). Bush was preparing his 1994 campaign for the Texas governorship. From Olasky, Bush learned an historical argument as to why government welfare programs can fail to redeem the poor.

According to Olasky, 19th-century religious charities were effective because they challenged recipients morally. Such charities, unafraid to make moral judgments, categorized the poor as deserving or undeserving. By focusing the most help on the deserving poor who retained their dignity and will to work, charities also gave an incentive to the undeserving poor for material and spiritual uplift.

But the 20th-century welfare state, as Olasky told the story, treated all of the poor as equally deserving of aid. It thereby left the undeserving poor with no incentive to uplift themselves. The welfare state reinforced rather than remedied the dependency of the undeserving poor.

Olasky's book concluded that government should get out of the way. We need, he said, to return to a world where care for the needy is a private and religious concern. But Olasky's book has absolutely nothing to say about the idea of direct government funding for faith-based initiatives which is the heart of Bush's program.

It was probably Bush with his managerial mindset who came up with the idea of government funding for faith-based initiatives. It was right and natural for Bush, as a Christian, to want to redeem Americans' characters and souls. But as a former businessman influenced by the idea of using values to lead, he also wanted to use faith-based organizations (FBOs) to improve the effectiveness of social service programs. He seems not to have seen the danger in trying to use faith for a secular purpose.

The crucial moment for Bush came in 1995 when, ensconced in the Texas governor's mansion, he found faith-based initiatives politically popular. An anti-addiction program called Teen Challenge used Christian counselors who did not meet state licensing requirements. Texas regulators tried to shut down Teen Challenge despite its claim of high cure rates for drug addicts.

Bush came to Teen Challenge's defense and pushed through the Texas legislature a bill exempting faith-based organizations from state licensing requirements. But it was a pyrrhic victory. That same legislation denied state funding to unlicensed organizations.

Despite the lack of state funding for FBOs like Teen Challenge, Bush represented his work as a triumph of faith. He of course sincerely believed that faith-based organizations could redeem ruined lives. But he did not miss the fact that his intervention had won him enormous popularity with Texas evangelicals.

Bush was moving with a national trend. In 1996 when Congress adopted the Clinton administration's welfare-to-work proposal, Senator John Ashcroft successfully attached a "Charitable Choice" provision to the law. Prior to Charitable Choice, religious groups had to apply for government social service grants via auxiliary organizations such as Catholic Charities, that is, auxiliary organizations with specifically charitable rather than religious objectives. But under Charitable Choice, churches, temples, and mosques can retain their religious character and apply for government funding to provide social services.

Charitable Choice did not authorize the use of tax dollars for religious purposes. Faith-based organizations were still supposed to respect church-state separation. They could get government grants for nonreligious social service but were not supposed to use the money to evangelize.

While Charitable Choice upheld separation of church and state in theory, it tore down the firewall that separated them in reality. Faith-based organizations could get government money but only for nonfaith purposes! Obviously, some FBOs would not be able to resist using taxpayers' dollars to spread their message.

And Charitable Choice could easily weaken the faith of religious groups who played by the rules. If they saw faith as the solution to drug addiction, they could get money to help drug addicts as long as they left out faith! The offer of government money might well tempt them to abandon their spiritual message!

Ashcroft's Charitable Choice was an untenable halfway house. It tempted zealous proselytizers to break the law separating church and state. And it tempted law-respecting people of faith to water down their message in order to get government money.

But Bush, as governor of Texas, was undiscouraged by the ambiguities in Charitable Choice. He issued executive orders and sponsored legislation to push state bureaucrats toward partnerships with federally funded FBOs. Operation of a Texas prison unit by an FBO became a well-known symbol of Bush's governorship.

Running for president in 2000, Bush had a strong record on faith-based initiatives at the state level with which he could appeal to evangelicals. Seeming to subscribe to values-based notions in the leadership cult, he announced in a 1999 speech that "We will never ask an organization to compromise its core values and spiritual mission."[9] It was clear that once in office Bush would not concern himself with upholding the fragile line separating church and state in Charitable Choice.

The little noticed danger in electing Bush was that his lax attitude on separation of church and state could corrupt the spirituality of the FBOs he meant to support. If FBOs lost sight of the prohibition on using federal money to spread the light, how could they be sure it was light rather than lucre that brought converts? How could they be sure that they were "faith based" rather than tax based? Or if they stuck to the letter of the law separating church and state, how could they be sure that they were not watering down their faith to get federal money?

Some evangelicals saw a solution to the latter problem in tax credits for charitable contributions. Under present tax law, only high earners who itemize deductions get a tax break for charitable gifts. Evangelicals therefore proposed a $500 income tax credit to reimburse low earners for charitable contributions. Such a credit would have diverted tax-payers' dollars from the federal government into evangelical charities where it could be spent with no concern for separation of church and state. Fundamentalist organizations like Teen Challenge would have been able to use such money to treat drug addicts without being required to take Jesus out of their therapy.

On the other hand, social scientists such as John Dilulio—who would become Bush's first director of Faith-Based Initiatives—favored continuing in the direction of Charitable Choice. Dilulio wanted to stay with what evangelicals such as Olasky disparagingly call "the grants economy." From Dilulio's social science perspective, the advantage of giving grants for specific purposes was the ability to evaluate results, allowing allocation of resources to the most effective programs.

The conflict was irresolvable. Evangelicals wanted to use good works to spread the word. Social scientists wanted to use the word to spread good works.

The 2000 Bush campaign mainly ignored the question of evangelicals versus social scientists. Bush's strategy was to say little at all about faith-based initiatives while letting Olasky and others reassure the religious right that major change was coming. During the 2000 campaign Olasky brought out a new book—*Compassionate Conservatism*—which evangelicals read as an implicit promise that Bush would expand government support for faith-based initiatives.

Bush's campaign strategy worked well. Evangelicals got the message that he would facilitate their access to federal money. And middle of the road voters remained largely unaware of Bush's plans for a change in church-state relations.

But as a result of Bush's campaign obscurity on faith-based initiatives, some big questions never got asked. What were the risks in Bush's program to religion itself? After all, the religious spirit has thrived in America under separation of church and state. Might government assistance to faith-based organizations make them less faith based and reduce their religious character? Bush seems never to have asked such questions.

Early in his first term Bush disappointed the evangelicals who favored tax credits as the solution to obtaining federal support for their programs. Instead, he submitted a bill to Congress that would have specifically applied the 1996 Charitable Choice law to numerous federal programs. The idea was to force government bureaucrats who had not understood or else resisted the 1996 law to obey it.

Some religious organizations opposed Bush's proposal. They saw as he evidently did not that his program threatened rather than supported their religious integrity. Even Teen Challenge, which had first stirred Bush's interest in faith-based organizations, feared that Bush's proposal would make it easier for the government "to interfere with our religious component."[10] Democrats, seeing that religious organizations were themselves divided over the issue, offered stiff opposition.

Stymied in Congress, Bush was nevertheless undiscouraged. He just went around the legislators. Falling back on his executive authority, Bush created dramatic change in church-state relations.

Bush ordered a study of FBOs' access to government grants. The resulting report, entitled "Unlevel Playing Field," was carelessly researched. It asserted, for example, that no grant money from the Department of Housing and Urban Development went to FBOs when, in fact, the Christian organization Habitat for Humanity was one of the department's largest grantees. But the report did demonstrate that the paperwork in the application process was forbidding to small organizations. And the report showed that some federal bureaucrats did not understand the 1996 Charitable Choice law.

The Bush administration used "Unlevel Playing Field" to justify action by the executive branch. It did not matter that Congress refused to act on Bush's proposed legislation. In fact, even before the report, Bush had taken action on his own to ensure that more government grants went to FBOs.

Soon after his inauguration, Bush had set up a White House Office of Faith-Based and Community Initiatives. He gave reach to that office by creating subordinate offices for faith-based initiatives within ten agencies and departments. And some other agencies set up, on their own, programs aimed at "leveling the playing field" for FBOs.

In effect Bush built a new, faith-based bureaucracy inside the federal government. Faith-based bureaucrats in each agency simplified application processes, made sure that federal officials understood Charitable Choice, and communicated the new approach to state governments which administer much of the social services money appropriated by Congress. The new faith-based bureaucrats used brochures, websites, and face to face meetings to reach out to FBOs and encourage them to apply for grants.

Bush's forceful approach got results. In 2003 five departments of the federal government—Health and Human Services, Housing and Urban Development, Labor, Justice, and Education—provided more than a billion dollars in grants to FBOs. And that total did not include state-administered federal funds that went to FBOs.

With the federal bureaucracy actively seeking to award grants to FBOs, the playing field had been not only leveled but, if anything, tilted in favor of religious groups. Bush permitted FBOs to practice religious discrimination in hiring to fill federally funded jobs. And he allowed buildings erected for social service work with taxpayers' dollars to be used for religious worship as well.

Some government meetings took on a tent-revival atmosphere. At a Washington conference where federal officials explained application processes to FBOs, a soloist sang "The Lord Jesus Deserves Our Praise." Then "100 faith-based providers rose to their feet, pumped their palms in the air, and chanted 'Amen' and 'Hallelujah.'"[11]

But it was not clear whether federal largesse was strengthening or weakening the religious spirit in faith-based organizations. In September 2003 Bill Moyers' PBS television program NOW presented a disturbing picture of the relationship between a Colorado FBO and a welfare mother. Using federal grant money, FBO volunteers helped the welfare mother prepare to return to school and also tutored her daughter.

For a few weeks the young mother, at her own initiative, attended the volunteers' church. But after skipping church for a few Sundays, she reported that she wished she hadn't gone in the first place: "… they told me, 'Oh, we're not gonna push church,' and this and that, but now it's been that issue, you know, of kind of pushing."[12]

Eventually, she returned to church. Perhaps it was for the sake of her children who needed the FBO's assistance. In any case, her remark that "it should have been of my own free will" makes clear that she felt her religious freedom was violated.[13]

Yet the woman also seemed drawn to the church. Perhaps it was the congregants' arm-twisting abuse of their federally funded power over her which led to her skipping a few Sundays. Bush's program of faith-based initiatives and the temptations for spiritual oppression it created may have held her back from embracing the church more enthusiastically, may have dampened rather than raised this woman's religious ardor.

What about the spirits of the Christians who twisted her arm? Were they really delivering their message in good faith? Or were they only deceiving themselves by running up a tally of dubious converts won via the power of government money?

Bush has made it harder for those Christians to search their hearts. Without Bush's program they could have achieved more assurance as to the purity of their motives in assisting that welfare mother. That's because they would have been spending their own money rather than the taxpayers'.

With huge amounts of welfare money now administered by FBOs, conditions are well suited for undemocratic violation of the religious freedom of our weakest and most vulnerable citizens. Even FBOs determined to obey the law are scarcely immune from power's power to corrupt or at least to desensitize. What seems like a gentle helping hand to the giver can have the appearance of a threat to weak and needy receivers.

Many believers understand the danger that government funding poses to their religious integrity. They will strive to retain their democratic understanding of why it is wrong to compel the consciences of others. Nevertheless, some with even the most scrupulous intentions will slip up and abuse their new federally funded power.

Bush's presidency, which some have seen as a victory for the religious spirit, is more likely a defeat. The evangelicals were right to distrust the social scientists with whom Bush ultimately sided. For just as values are subverted by trying to use them for ulterior purposes, so is religion.

Some among the Christian right have already recognized the spiritual damage that Bush's leadership has done to them. Intending to put politics to the service of religion, they have done the reverse. As one veteran of the Bush administration ruefully noted, they had forgotten "C. S. Lewis's caution never to let Christian faith become a means to an end but only an end itself."[14]

By politicizing religion on the right Bush has probably also increased secularization on the left. Even before Bush came to power there was plenty of evidence that harshly aggressive right-wing evangelicalism was pushing many Americans toward distaste for institutional religion.[15] Faith-based initiatives can only have exacerbated that tendency.

Since Bush's program of faith-based initiatives has been a sort of giant experiment in spirituality at work, its bitter lessons apply not just to government but to business as well. The danger that using spirituality as a leadership tool will subvert spirituality is probably even greater in the corporate world than in government. Government funding for faith-based initiatives goes mainly to religions with a tradition of warning against false pride. But the movement for spirituality at work draws not just on religion but on the cult of moral leadership which, rather than warning against false pride, encourages it.

Faith-based initiatives and Sarbanes-Oxley would have been more than sufficient lessons as to the hurtful consequences of the cult of moral leadership. Unfortunately, George Bush has provided one more major example of the leadership cult's moral dangers. To the worst attack on the United States in half a century, he responded by attempting to use values to lead, only to launch an unconstitutional war on terror.

Chapter 8

The Unconstitutional War on Terror

Everything that is wrong with the leadership cult gets worse during times of major change. To navigate in a slow stream is one thing, white water rapids another. As the danger of capsizing increases, so does the illusion that values are life jackets.

In reality, it's the other way round. As the water gets rougher our values are more likely to be swamped. The more turbulent the change the more our values need to be buoyed by ethical understanding, situational knowledge, and professional competence.

Our moral danger is even graver when we face an evil change. There is truth in the hackneyed movie plot about the cop who, in order to catch a sociopath, becomes one himself. When we seem to be on the side of the angels, we are still vulnerable to the devil's wiles.

An attack by evildoers is therefore no guarantee that we will not respond with wrongdoing of our own. In the aftermath of the obviously evil 9/11 attacks, George W. Bush also did wrong. He unconstitutionally declared war on terror.

In a speech to the nation on the evening of 9/11, Bush spoke, almost in passing, of a "war against terrorism." It was as if all that was required to take us to war was his three-word mention of it. Franklin Roosevelt, after Pearl Harbor, asked Congress to declare war. Bush declared war all by himself, violating his inaugural oath to uphold the Constitution of the United States.

The Constitution says that "Congress," not the President, "shall have power ... to declare war." And Congress did not declare war on terrorism after 9/11. Instead, on September 14, Congress passed a resolution authorizing Bush to use force against "those nations, organizations, or persons he determines planned, authorized, committed, or aided the terrorist attacks that occurred on September 11, 2001."

Congress clearly limited Bush's military response to those who had attacked us on 9/11. Yet Bush says we are engaged in a "global" war on all terror. He usurped Congress's constitutional authority to declare war.

As far as I can find, Bush has dealt only once with the fact that he has no congressional authorization for a global war on terror. In a television interview with Barbara Walters not long after 9/11, he said that he had "felt no need" for a congressional declaration of war. This is the simplistic moral philosophy of the leadership cult, which makes so much of personal values and feelings, so little of facts.

The United States has long experience with undeclared wars. But until now, wars that Congress did not declare were not thought of as wars at the start. They began as seemingly small-scale conflicts which the president hoped would not last long or at least not grow large.

The Civil War is an exception. Although Congress never declared war, Lincoln and others warned against "civil war" before hostilities began. But as the suppression of a domestic rebellion, the Civil War is in a special class.

Of course our many conflicts with Native Americans were often called "wars" in popular speech. But like other undeclared wars, they were small scale at the start. And like the Civil War, these conflicts took place within our own borders.

When we have previously fought undeclared wars against foreign powers, presidents have not believed it was war at the outset. The Korean War, described as a United Nations "police action" at the start, would have been over within months if China had not intervened on behalf of the North Koreans. For the Vietnam War it is impossible to specify the exact date on which we were no longer just "advising" but fighting a war of our own.

A century ago when we suppressed an independence movement in the Philippines, no one knew at the start that it would turn into a four-year guerilla war. A century before that we fought, against France, a "quasi-war" which Congress would have happily declared at the start. But President John Adams' refusal to ask Congress for a declaration of war helped him achieve his goal of limiting the conflict.

Whenever previous presidents have believed that it was a matter of war at the start, they have asked Congress to declare it. Presidents

Madison, Polk, McKinley, Wilson, and Roosevelt asked Congress to declare, respectively, the War of 1812, the Mexican War, the Spanish American War, World War I, and World War II. Bush's father, President George H. W. Bush, had to be pressured to do it, but he asked Congress to authorize the 1991 Gulf War after Iraq invaded Kuwait.

George Bush is the first president who believed it was a matter of war at the outset who has not asked Congress to authorize it. Instead, he declared a global war on terror all by himself. It is the first presidentially declared war in American history.

All previous wars in American history were either declared or undeclared. Bush has muddled the two categories. By declaring an undeclared war he has violated the Constitution he swore to protect.

It is not necessarily wrong to violate the Constitution. When Lincoln was accused of unconstitutionally suspending the writ of habeas corpus during the Civil War, he asked, "Are all the laws but one to go unexecuted ... lest that one be violated?"[1] A century later Supreme Court Justice Robert Jackson said that the Constitution "is not a suicide pact." If in a time of great national danger the President can better defend the country by violating the Constitution, he or she should do so.

So Bush's one-man declaration of war was not necessarily wrong just because it was unconstitutional. The question is whether Bush's violation of the Constitution increased his ability to defend the country in a time of grave danger. The answer is no.

The immediate danger was from the 9/11 terrorists. And on September 14 Congress gave Bush authority to use "all necessary and appropriate force" against them. So if Bush wanted a global war on terrorism, there was no national danger preventing him from taking the time to ask Congress to declare that global war rather than to violate the Constitution by doing so himself.

Bush's usurpation of the power to declare war shows how a leader can unwittingly subvert the values he invokes. Bush believed he was defending freedom. But he breached the constitutional separation of powers between executive and legislature by which the founders aimed to protect freedom.

Bush's violation of the Constitution was not only unnecessary and wrong, it was hurtful to our national defense. If he had obeyed the Constitution, he could have done a better job of fighting terrorism.

Obeying the law would have forced Bush to use more than values to lead. He would have been forced into hands-on management. Just preparing to ask Congress to declare war might have improved the administration's rationality and helped it see why, for reasons explained below, a war on terror was a strategic mistake.

Or if the administration had still requested a declaration of war, then Congress could have sorted out the issues. If Congress had declared a global war on terror, Bush would have preserved his moral standing by obeying the law. If Congress had refused Bush's request for a declaration of war, he might have more carefully weighed subsequent decisions on Iraq.

Congress and the public also failed in their responsibility. Since Congress on September 14 had granted the president power to punish only the 9/11 terrorists, it should have explicitly rejected Bush's declaration of a global war on terror. But Congress was frightened by Bush's soaring poll numbers, which in turn amounted to a failure of responsibility on the part of the public.

Yet Bush committed the initial offense. His moral failure in declaring war all by himself preceded and helped cause a moral failure by Congress and the public, not vice versa. The moral quality of leadership does matter.

Many attribute Bush's moral errors and violations of the Constitution to hubris. Others see sincerity in his belief that presidential power needs strengthening. Both these factors are probably part of the truth.

But Bush's grasp for unwarranted power was also consistent with being insufficiently on guard against insidious temptations inherent in leadership. With the people rallying round him in a time of danger while he used values to lead, Bush was exposed to the temptation to imagine himself a moral exemplar. Launching a war of good against evil, he may have succumbed to the risk of false pride.

September 11 collapsed into a day the same temptations Bush had faced at Harken Energy in the spring of 1990. In both cases there were factors that could have undermined whatever defenses he had against self-righteousness. His good work at Harken in fending off wrongdoing to small shareholders could have helped him justify, to himself, his morally mistaken stock sale. Similarly, the obvious evil of the 9/11 attacks could have lowered his guard against the moral danger in taking up the role of self-conscious moral leader.

Adding to the temptation to take false pride in moral leadership was the fact that before 9/11 Bush seemed headed for a lackluster presidency. His tax and education proposals were mundane policy, not the sort of large historical issues affecting national identity that are characteristic of an important presidency. Bush seemed to deserve the same hollow-at-the-core criticism that had dogged his father; he had no vision.

Few presidents have seemed less like charismatic leaders in their first eight months in office than George W. Bush. A month-long vacation in Texas in August 2001 had solidified his drifting, do-nothing image. As September 11 approached, polls put his approval ratings at 51 percent, a low for a new president surpassed only by Gerald Ford when he pardoned Richard Nixon.[2]

Then came the 9/11 attacks to which Bush's initial response was unimpressive. He was in Florida that morning, preparing to push his education plan with a photo op in a second-grade classroom. His advisors informed him of what seemed a terrible accident—a jetliner had struck the North Tower of the World Trade Center in lower Manhattan.

Bush then joined the second graders for a reading lesson. As the children read aloud and the cameras rolled, the president's chief of staff walked up to him, whispered that a second plane had struck the South Tower, and added, "America is under attack."

And then the president went back to listening to the children read a story about a pet goat. After bantering with the kids, he posed for photos with the teacher. Somewhere between seven and nine minutes after learning of the attack, he finally left the classroom to deal with the crisis.

Bush later insisted that he was thinking decisively while sitting with the seven-year-olds: "I made up my mind at that moment that we were going to war."[3] It would be strange if he had not thought of the possibility of war. But it would also have been rash of him to have made up his mind on war before he knew who had attacked and why.

Of course, it is more likely that Bush decided nothing in those first moments but was just sitting frozen in shock. But either way, his claim that he settled on war while listening to second graders suggests a mistaken notion of decisiveness. Bush says he made up his mind when he had only a vague knowledge of the situation.

Whether or not Bush immediately decided on war when he heard of the attacks, he rashly made up his mind within hours. According to Bob Woodward, Bush repeated to his aides all day on September 11 that the attacks were an "act of war." Treasury Secretary Paul O'Neill remembered a White House meeting on September 13 where the only question was "whether this was a war against al Qaeda and its host,

Afghanistan's Taliban regime, or the first step in a struggle against worldwide terrorism."[4]

In other words, by September 13, the only question on Bush's mind was not whether we were at war, but with whom; and he seems to have thought that answer was up to him alone. There is no indication that he paid attention to the fact that Congress on the next day, September 14, authorized him to fight only al Qaeda and those who aided it. Bush was ready to fight a global war on terror without congressional authorization.

Neither did Bush seem to notice that in its September 14 resolution, Congress avoided the word "war" even against al Qaeda. Some in Congress probably knew something that Bush could have usefully learned from them. Contrary to what Bush said all day on September 11, a terrorist attack is not an act of war. Wars are fought between states, not between terrorists and a state.

The crucial distinction in international law is between sovereign states and lesser actors. A terrorist attack would be an act of war only if it were sponsored by a state. The 9/11 atrocities, according to a December 2001 legal report commissioned by Congress, "were not 'acts of war' in the traditional sense, because the perpetrators were not overtly acting on behalf of a state."[5]

Some legal theorists have tried to furnish a rationale for Bush's mistaken war on terror by arguing that al Qaeda is a quasi-military force. Others have suggested that support for al Qaeda by the Afghani state qualifies the September 11 attacks as an act of war. Yet another argument is that since the United States is a sovereign state, its military response made the attack, after the fact, an act of war.[6]

Against such arguments is the fact that many other nations have had long experience with terrorism without declaring war on it. Israel, with over half a century of experience fighting terrorism, has never declared war on it. England and Spain have treated IRA and Basque terrorists not as warriors but as criminals.

Since 9/11 some Bush partisans have mocked the idea of fighting terrorists as criminals. They say we would be fighting with our hands tied behind our backs, reading Miranda rights to suicide bombers. But of course criminal statutes and procedures have often changed in the past to meet new needs.

Others have proposed that terrorism can only be dealt with as its own legal category, neither crime nor war. Some politicians are trying to back away from the "war on terror" by suggesting that the phrase is a metaphor. In 2005 some members of the Bush administration floated the idea of dropping the name "war on terror" as misleading. But Bush overruled them: "Make no mistake about it, we are at war."[7]

Bush means "war" literally, not figuratively. To him the war on terror is not a metaphor like the "war on poverty" or the "war on drugs." He sees the war on terror as real war, which is what makes his unilateral declaration of it unconstitutional.

Bush's illegal declaration of war has made him less, not more, effective as a leader. He could have better slaked his thirst for top-down moral leadership by explaining to the American people why "war" was the wrong response to terrorism. By avoiding war fever his administration might have avoided its later jingoistic rhetoric and the damage it did to America's reputation.

By declaring war on terror, Bush raised the prestige of al Qaeda. In effect, he supported their claim that they were soldiers, not murderers. Al Qaeda's status could only rise from being thought worthy of war by the world's most powerful nation.

"War" is also the wrong strategy for fighting terrorism because such a war can never be won with certainty. It is possible to defeat a nation, but terrorism is an action. We can never know that we have created a world where there will be no terrorist actions.

In World War II, for example, we fought a war that could be won because Germany, Japan, and Italy were nation states with armies that could be destroyed, governments that could be removed, and territories that could be occupied. But if we had responded to Pearl Harbor by declaring war on the action of sneak attackism,[8] just as Bush has declared war on the action of terrorism, we would probably still be at war. In fact, September 11 would have been just the latest defeat in our ill conceived "war" against sneak attackism.

The day that Bush or one of his successors declares victory over terrorism, some madman may detonate a bomb just to prove the president wrong. The war against terror will not end with any final victory over terrorists. It will only end when we sensibly stop waging "war" against terrorism while continuing to fight it.

But the word "war" probably had deep appeal to Bush as a leadership tool. People rally to a leader in war, at least at the start. And a war against terrorism had a ring of righteousness that Bush could have seen as useful in leading by values.

With his long practice of using values to lead, Bush inevitably tried to manage the war against terrorism by values. Speaking to the nation on 9/11, he said that the terrorists had attacked because they "hate freedom." Although al Qaeda surely does hate many aspects of open societies, the main motivation for the 9/11 attacks seems to have been to protest American troops in Saudi Arabia.[9]

Bush's post-9/11 rhetoric veered dangerously toward moral grandiosity. There is no disputing his statement on 9/11 that the attacks were "evil." But the next day he spoke apocalyptically of a "monumental struggle of good against evil."[10] And Bush already knew the struggle's outcome. Good, he assured us, would triumph in the end.

On September 14, at the National Cathedral, Bush said that America's "responsibility to history is already clear: to answer these attacks and rid the world of evil." The rid-the-world-of-evil rhetoric was surprising from a president who wears his Christianity on his sleeve. Christians have traditionally held that human beings should fight evil but not expect to rid themselves entirely of it. Bush was showing signs of forgetting the part of his religious tradition he most needed—humility.

Of course Bush is perfectly capable of sitting at a White House luncheon for neo-conservative intellectuals and discussing the proposition that it is dangerous for the "pious to be too moralistic and careless in speaking of good and evil."[11] But such heady discussions are what Aristotle called "intellectual virtue." The real test is in action, practice, and habit, which the ancient philosopher called "moral virtue."

It is one thing to agree intellectually to the danger of false pride. It is another thing really to guard against it. And it was probably harder still for Bush since his Christian faith had to contend with the danger of false pride from his corporate practice of using values to lead.

On September 20 Bush, speaking to Congress, said that al Qaeda attacked us because they "hate what we see right here in this chamber—a democratically elected government." Yet almost in the next breath he disrespected the elected legislators in front of him. Their September 14 resolution had limited his use of force to al Qaeda, but Bush in effect overrode their decision, telling them that the "war on terror" would "not end until every terrorist group of global reach has been found, stopped and defeated."

There are few better examples of a leader violating values he proclaims than Bush's post-9/11 attempt at moral leadership. He tried to rally followers around the value of freedom. But he was violating the Constitution that protected freedom.

Bush sounded relieved as he announced that "We have found our mission and our moment." He evidently believed that he had found an escape from the leadership problem that had dogged his father—"the vision thing." He would leave his presidential doldrums behind him by using good values to fight evil.

Confidence that victory is mainly a matter of values is an understandable temptation to a leader at the start of a war. National unity against an external enemy makes it easier to lead in war than in peace, at least at the start, before a war's costs are understood. The great 20th-century political scientist Mary Parker Follett said that war is "a kind of rest-cure" compared to the moral challenge of governing in peacetime.[12]

Taking up with relish the role of moral leader in the war on terror, Bush sought to expand the war. He later said that after September 11, his Defense Secretary, Donald Rumsfeld, "wisely—and I agreed with this—was looking for other places where we could show that the war on terror was global."[13] When Secretary of State Colin Powell pointed out that a global war on terror could cost us allies against al Qaeda, Bush replied that "At some point, we may be the only ones left. That's okay with me. We are America."[14]

Bush's prophecy of virtuous isolation ran the risk of fulfilling itself. Most other nations abhor terrorism. The off putting moral arrogance in the belief we might have to stand alone could help drive away potential friends.

The job of alienating friends got underway in earnest in June 2002. In a commencement speech at West Point, Bush announced a new strategy of military "preemption." And the following September he laid out the case for preemption in a state paper, *The National Security Strategy of the United States of America*.

Bush's preemptive strategy defied Congress, which had previously rejected his request for such power. Immediately after 9/11, Bush had asked Congress for authority to "preempt any future acts of terrorism or aggression against the United States."[15] But Congress remembered too well how Lyndon Johnson had claimed authority for the Vietnam War under the Gulf of Tonkin resolution.

Therefore, Congress had refused to enact the broad and vague power Bush had requested. Instead, Congress stated in its September 14 resolution that the President already had authority to "deter and prevent" terrorist attacks. Congress clearly meant to deny Bush the authority he had requested to "preempt any ... aggression" he believed he saw coming.

Yet in his September 2002 paper on *National Security Strategy*, Bush ignored, forgot, or maybe never knew that Congress had earlier denied his request for permission to preempt aggression any time he chose. He announced a policy of preemptive attacks against "rogue states." And he would preemptively strike them "even if uncertainty remains as to the time and place of the enemy's attack."

Bush justified preemption pragmatically. The policy of containment and deterrence that had won the Cold War would not work against terrorism. Terror, knowing no borders, cannot be contained. Fanatics in search of martyrdom will not be deterred by the "mutual assured destruction" that kept peace with the Soviet Union.

Since it is all too imaginable that Bush was right that situations will arise where preemption is the only sensible course, it is a fair question why the rest of the world gasped in alarm. Worldwide, the media were filled with stories about America's dangerous new security policy. Although Bush vowed to defend allies, some of them were among the nations most worried.

Our friends' fear resulted at least partly from Bush's failure to understand the moral danger of a preemptive foreign policy. He gave no hint of awareness that America's power endangered America's character. In fact, his self-righteousness suggested that the damage had been done.

Instead of stating that preemption might be a terrible necessity, Bush justified preemption with moral arrogance. It was all right for America to preempt, Bush said in his paper on *National Security Strategy*, because "we do not use our strength to press for unilateral advantage." How unreasonable of others not to take our word for it!

By now Bush was taking himself very seriously—and very foolishly— as a moral preceptor. In his June 2002 West Point speech he had tried to head off charges of moral danger in preemption by invoking "moral clarity." Virtue is clear, he obtusely claimed, because "Moral truth is the same in every culture, in every time and in every place."

His example of universal moral truth—"murder is always and everywhere wrong"—was indisputable. But not everyone agrees as to when a killing is murder. If Bush were to kill innocent people in a preemptive attack, he might call it collateral damage, but their loved ones would likely call it murder.

Bush was embarrassingly out of his depth in these inch-deep philo-sophical waters. Even if there is such a thing as universal moral truth, its universality means it must be very general. And human beings know from long, painful experience that general moral ideas can be difficult to apply to specific situations. With his sophomoric philosophizing, Bush looked like some intolerant truth monger, with the scary differ-ence that he was the most powerful man in the world.

By mistaking moral arrogance for moral leadership and announcing a general policy of preemption, Bush dissipated the good will that the world offered the United States after September 11. Turning sympathy for America into fear, he brought the country's standing in the world to a low unknown since Vietnam. Considering the fact that we had been attacked, it was an astonishing reversal.

At home, however, Bush's moral influence as a war president had surged. He used his new prestige to push for a preemptive invasion of Iraq. In October 2002 Congress authorized force if diplomacy did not persuade Saddam Hussein to give up the weapons of mass destruction he supposedly possessed. By asking for permission to attack Iraq, Bush made his actions legal but not his words. Congress gave him authority to fight. But he had no authority for the global war on terror of which he said Iraq was only a part.

The fact that Bush's illegal behavior was verbal does not mean that it did no tangible harm. To many citizens his global war on terror made the preemptive invasion of Iraq seem like a logical follow-up to going after Osama bin Laden in Afghanistan. The war atmosphere made it harder for the public and Congress to weigh the evidence on how large a threat Saddam Hussein really was to the United States.

Bush himself may have been a victim of his war rhetoric. Although it is widely believed that Bush manipulated intelligence to deceive us into the Iraq War, the reality may be more complicated. He may have deceived himself into war.

Until 9/11 Bush seems to have had control of his administration's extremists on Iraq. Even until the summer of 2002, according to the best investigative journalism on the subject, Bush was not entirely com-mitted to invading Iraq.[16] But his war rhetoric convinced subordinates that he had made up his mind.

Adding to government bureaucrats' conviction that the Bush admin-istration had already decided to invade Iraq was Vice President Cheney's attempt to establish a nonexistent link between Saddam Hussein and the 9/11 attacks. Cheney seemed to be attempting to create a legal basis for invading Iraq without congressional approval. If Saddam Hussein could be connected to 9/11, Bush could claim that Congress had already approved an attack on Iraq when it authorized force against the 9/11 terrorists. Although Cheney hoodwinked a large part of the public, Congress was not deceived.

So administration hawks fell back on weapons of mass destruction. The September 2002 National Intelligence Estimate that stretched the evidence on Iraq's weapons of mass destruction (WMD) probably aimed to give Bush what the CIA thought he wanted. Thanks to the stretched evidence, "Bush's view became that CIA director George Tenet says they have WMD, and Cheney says don't get caught napping again like we did on 9/11."[17] The bureaucratic echo of his war rhetoric may have cost Bush his chance of understanding that Iraq posed little immediate threat.

Once settled on the invasion, Bush might have been expected to have planned the post-war occupation with care. In his 2000 campaign, he had fiercely criticized "state building" as unrealistic. Now, having embraced "regime change" for Iraq, he was embarked on just such a project.

Yet despite Bush's past skepticism on state building there was little planning for the post-war occupation of Iraq. An investigation led by former Defense Secretary James Schlesinger "concluded there had been a failure not only to plan for an insurgency, but also to react to the insurgency once it erupted."[18] Planning had been limited to the military campaign, leaving a disconnect between the fighting and its goal of democratizing Iraq.

Bush overlooked the occupation and the insurgency because he looked past them, which was probably what he thought a visionary leader should do. What mattered to him was his vision of Iraq as a "game changer."[19] He believed that the invasion would instill fear in other dubious regimes and end their support for terrorists.

But without competent planning Iraq could not change the game. Even before the invasion, the Bush administration alienated many Iraqis by working with the expatriate carpet bagger Ahmed Chalabi. As for the invasion itself, the Bush administration sent enough troops to topple Saddam Hussein but not enough to secure the country. The insurgency then tied down the American military, opened Shiite Iraq to influence by Shiite Iran, rallied Sunnis to the support of diehard Baathists, and drew in al Qaeda sympathizers and jihadists from other nations.

How did Bush commit such a colossal blunder? His seeming ability to deny facts in front of his nose has gotten a lot of discussion ever since one of his White House aides was quoted in 2004 as disparaging the "reality-based community."[20] The popular and probably correct notion is that Bush's predilection for "righteous action—such as attacking evil or spreading 'God's gift' of freedom" distinguished his decision-making style from the "shades-of-gray analysis that has been a staple of most presidents' diets."[21]

But if Bush has a reality problem, it probably originates at least partly in his practice of using values to lead. A values-based, visionary leader is supposed to look at the horizon and beyond, not at the facts on the ground. However deeply Bush's decision-making style may originate in personal narcissism and wishful denial, he probably finds intellectual support for it in the cult of moral leadership. Mundane managerial work like planning is not the job of the moral leader.

Bush's penchant for leading by values—not just the fact, as Bob Woodward points out, that he had been a prep school cheerleader—accounted for there being "little or no evidence that he engaged in much substantive policy debate at this point [2003] in the war cabinet meetings." The hard work of planning the invasion and managing the occupation could be left to others. Bush seems to have believed his "role was to express confidence and enthusiasm."[22]

One risk of leading by cheering is that subordinates will do likewise. Paul Bremer—in charge of occupying and rebuilding Iraq—lauded Bush's "grandeur of vision."[23] He got the job of running the occupation after a brief Oval Office meeting in which he told Bush that his wife admired the president's declaration that "Freedom is not America's gift to the world. It is God's gift to mankind."[24]

Like Bush, Bremer was a Harvard MBA accustomed to the big-picture rhetoric of moral leadership. The key test of fitness to help Bremer rebuild Iraq was whether the candidate shared "the President's vision for Iraq."[25] Not surprisingly, Bremer's administration of Iraq included more than its fair share of incompetents such as the 24-year-old with White House connections but no finance background who was assigned to rebuild the Baghdad stock exchange.[26]

Managing by values, Bremer bungled the major decision of the occupation. Out of understandable disgust for the Baathist Party, he mistakenly disbanded the Iraqi army and fired thousands of senior civil servants, driving resentful Sunnis into the insurgency. The United States was left to try to build a new army for Iraq from the ground up in the middle of a civil war.

As the situation in Iraq grew grim, Bush betrayed no second thoughts. Iraq, he said in an inapt metaphor from set-piece warfare, is the "central front" in the war on terror. Any number of times Bush has said of Iraq that he "would have done it again."[27]

Bush may really have convinced himself that he would have done it again. But even if he truly believes that he would do it again, one hopes for his sake that the statement is, unconsciously, the sort of lie into which, as Machiavelli said, politics can push the prince. No leader of sense and decency would have invaded Iraq if he had known, as Bush knows now, that Saddam Hussein had no weapons of mass destruction and that removing him would be immensely costly.

The invasion of Iraq has cost, at the time I write, the lives of 3,600 American service men and women plus more than 1,000 civilian contractors, more people than were killed on 9/11. Hundreds of other troops from our coalition partners have also died. Tens of thousands more soldiers have been physically and psychologically maimed. They will rightly collect disability benefits for the rest of their lives.

Since 2003 Congress has appropriated more than $500 billion for the Iraq War. The total monetary cost, including future benefits for veterans, is certain to surpass a trillion dollars. Combined with Bush's insistence on low taxes, the Iraq War has led to massive borrowing and weakened our long-term economic security.

Terrible as our costs are, Iraq's are far greater. The UN High Commissioner for Refugees estimates that 2.1 million Iraqis have fled to neighboring countries. In addition, 1.9 million Iraqis still in the country have lost their homes.[28] If our population—11 times as big as Iraq's—had suffered proportionally, 23 million Americans would be refugees in Canada and Mexico, while another 21 million still in the United States would have been displaced from their homes.

Late in 2005 Bush estimated that "30,000 [Iraqis], more or less, have died as a result of the initial incursion and the ongoing violence,"[29] an estimate the White House later said was based on media accounts rather than any official attempt by the administration to learn how costly the invasion had been in terms of Iraqi lives. But a scientific study published in the *Lancet* concluded that in the first 40 months after the invasion, 655,000 Iraqis died from violence or from disease due to the destruction of water and sewer systems, electricity shortages, and the flight of health professionals.[30] Using Bush's estimate as the low end and the *Lancet* study as the high end, we can calculate that Iraq's population—1/11th the size of ours—suffered losses over roughly a three-year period proportional to what we would have endured from an invasion and occupation that took the lives of between 330,000 and 7 million Americans.

A leader's denial of responsibility for such horror can be consistent with managing by values and with a corollary and reckless disregard for reality. Bush understandably refuses to admit that his war was a catastrophic error for both Iraq and for us. The results of his mistaken war are not all in, but we may one day consider it a parallel to the Balkan Wars that a century ago preceded World War I—i.e., a mere prelude to even greater disaster.

Of course, no one knows what the future holds. It is possible that some good will come from the Iraq War. History contains greater ironies.

But if humanity's huge losses in the Iraq War are someday seen to have been partially offset by its having done some good, Bush will deserve no credit for it. The good would be a matter of moral luck, not moral leadership. At the time of his decision, he had no evidence that came close to justifying the harm that the invasion has done. And he probably has no clue that all this hurt originated in his unconstitutional declaration of a global war on terror.

It is impossible to know how Bush justifies his actions to himself. But his public statements as to why he pushes on with the war in Iraq are consistent with the cult of moral leadership. As his war grows ever more costly in blood and treasure, Bush gives the appearance of serenely believing that his behavior is principled. He even claims as a virtue his disregard for polls showing that Americans have joined the rest of the world in favoring a U.S. withdrawal from Iraq. After all, a moral leader should be guided by values alone.

Conclusion: Earn Moral Influence, Don't Use It

George W. Bush's failed presidency has had at least one good result. He has demonstrated the danger of the leadership cult. He has shown that using values to lead is a poor prescription for moral leadership.

The prescription can be improved only by recognizing that it takes more than good values to be a moral leader. It takes moral influence. Leaders are worthy of moral influence to the degree that they work *for* values, not *use* them.

Any fundamentally important value can only be a goal, not a tool. A corporate executive who wants to be a moral leader needs to treat integrity not as a way to make money but as a goal more important than profit. A president who wants to be a moral leader has to treat his oath to uphold the Constitution as a goal more important than political prestige.

Real moral leaders such as Mahatma Gandhi and Martin Luther King did not use fundamental values like freedom and equality to make themselves great. They became great by working *for* such fundamental values as freedom and equality. Followers, seeing that Gandhi and King competently upheld values they shared, accorded them moral influence.

Moral influence is a little like the money that parents save for their children's education. Parents earn the money. Their children use it.

Leaders can earn moral influence. But only followers can rightly use it. When a leader proposes a venture, potential followers audit, so to speak, the leader's moral bank account to see if they want to invest themselves.

Leaders make deposits in their moral bank accounts by helping followers achieve their values. That's why it is wrong to separate managerial competence from inspirational leadership. Competence helps leaders to manage effectively for values and thereby obtain moral influence. Competence and charisma are mutually reinforcing.

Therefore, Machiavelli's ideas have meaning for leaders who would like to achieve not just the appearance but the reality of virtue. Since Machiavelli was right that dishonesty is sometimes a competitive advantage, honest leaders need to find offsetting advantages of their own. Superior competence is even more vital to success for honest leaders than dishonest ones.

Competence was integral to the original conception of charisma. Today's tendency to think of charisma as a personality trait is contrary to the concept of charismatic leadership as it was created by the great social scientist Max Weber. He saw charisma as dependent on achievement, not just personality.

Weber called charisma a "quality of an individual personality ... treated as endowed with supernatural ... qualities."[1] The key word is not "personality" but "treated." It is not enough to be born with a charming personality. To be a leader, followers must recognize one's charisma.

Followers treat those people as charismatic whom they believe worthy of it. In traditional societies, Weber said, charisma is accorded "to prophets, to people with a reputation for therapeutic or legal wisdom, to leaders in the hunt, and heroes in war."[2] It takes not just personality and values but results to win charisma that lasts.

Therefore, charisma cannot long survive failure. "Even the old Germanic kings," Weber said, "were sometimes rejected with scorn."[3] No matter how magnetic the personality, followers will withdraw charisma from a leader who does not get results. The extraordinary drop in Bush's approval ratings from the high 80s after 9/11 to the mid-20s as a result of his incompetence in Iraq confirms Weber's observation.

Now that many of Bush's followers have treated him like one of Weber's old Germanic kings, withdrawing his charisma and rejecting him with scorn, there is a natural tendency to look for villains behind the throne. But even if Vice President Cheney has been the master manipulator that his critics make him out to be, Bush would still be guilty of foolishly relinquishing power to a subordinate. His failed presidency is at least partly due to his tendency to forgo the use of competence in favor of values to lead.

An executive eager to be a genuinely charismatic and moral leader should therefore use power to get results by managing *for* values. Such a leader should treat values as goals and then try to act competently to achieve those goals. By thinking of values as goals, we improve our chance of staying focused on right actions. Bush has gone wrong by thinking of values as tools, not goals.

Bush's resulting failure suggests how mistaken is leadership gurus' tendency to focus narrowly on personal psychological development as the path to moral leadership. Such leadership development programs probably do produce better people with more balanced psyches. But they leave out the essential ethical understanding needed for moral caution; the values we state are at best goals that often cannot be achieved and that can only be approached through situational knowledge and professional competence.

Leaders who manage *for* values have a good, though hardly foolproof, safeguard against moral grandiosity. To manage for values is to acknowledge that no one can state his or her values with certainty. One can only say what one hopes to value when the moment of action arrives.

Managing *for* values is a good—though again, not foolproof—safeguard against corruption. By thinking of values as goals to be met through action, leaders are less likely to slip into the complacency and false pride that can lead to moral ruin. If George Bush had been less certain that he knew what he valued and more focused on treating values as goals, he might have been more cautious both about selling his Harken Energy stock and about invading Iraq.

Treating values as goals is also consistent with rejecting the unrealistic moral optimism of the leadership cult. As chapter 5 established, some degree of immorality is an inescapable part of leadership. A leader has a better chance of acting as morally as possible by realistically recognizing the difficulty of achieving values instead of fatuously claiming to have them.

For what values goals should a leader manage? Values goals are often explicit or at least implicit in organizations. The circumstances will be rare where followers need to be led toward values goals different from those toward which they already should aspire.

The President, for example, has a moral guide in the Constitution. It expresses the value of peace and the moral danger of leadership by giving Congress, not the President, the power to declare war. Bush disrespected the Constitution and started himself on a disastrous path, both morally and practically, by usurping Congress's power and single-handedly declaring a global war on terror.

So at least part of the answer to how a leader should find values goals is to look at his or her organization and followers. Checking one's gut and stating one's own supposedly heartfelt values are not good enough. The long established values goals of the organization and its people, both explicit and implicit, also need consideration.

Our co-workers' values goals can be read not only in their words but in their behavior and the organization's behavior. That behavior can always be improved. But it is a rare case where values goals need to be revolutionized.

Life often requires great change of us. But that change is more often in the way we achieve our goals than in the goals themselves. A leader who tries to manage by values and to revolutionize followers' values goals is less likely a moral leader than an immoral one.

By his confidence in his values as moral guides, Bush has fallen into wrongdoing. As one would expect from a person overly confident that he knows himself and his values, Bush seems to have become careless of the need to examine his actions. And as Aristotle said, it is only by right actions that we acquire the habit of virtue.

Bush's example of overindulging in values talk at the expense of doing the right thing offers a lesson to business leaders. The first step for businesses who want to manage *for* values is to get rid of their "values statements." Companies who naively state their values violate, just as Bush has done, both the wisdom of religious tradition and the science of modern psychology, according to which the heart is difficult to know. Business leaders can help save themselves from Bush-style failure by stating "values goals" and then trying to assess their performance in achieving those goals, the same as they do for earnings.

Business ethics and business profits are similar in at least one way. We should never rest on past performance. Stating values as if they are a done deal is like saying that investors should be concerned only with last year's earnings.

Just as we should get rid of values statements in business, we should get rid of them in politics. Candidates who do not state their values but, rather, speak of them as goals are more likely to focus on doing the right thing. They are also less likely to subvert values by trying to use them for ulterior purposes.

But even though we should get rid of values statement in politics, we won't. Values statements, as Bush has shown, are too useful to leaders in distracting voters from incompetent performance. He is not the first and will not be the last politician to engage in excessive values talk. Just as Machiavelli said, moral pretense will always be part of political leadership.

The same is true of the corporate world where Bush probably first encountered the idea of using values to lead. Because immoral methods sometimes succeed, managing by values will not go away. Therefore, in business no less than in the political arena, many will cling to the leadership cult, especially those who, like Bush, mistakenly see it as a path to virtue.

Yet some other leaders would like to understand, really, the moral challenges of their jobs. Some will realistically accept the fact that genuinely moral leadership may require more, not less, competence and hard work to achieve high performance. Such worthy managers deserve a more realistic understanding of ethics than is provided in the leadership cult.

And our democracy needs a morally more realistic understanding of corporate culture. It is well known that corporate financial and political power are challenges to democracy in a global economy. But morally unrealistic corporate culture is a still greater threat because it more insidiously undermines democratic culture.

So even though the cult of moral leadership will never be defeated, it must be opposed. The fact that it cannot be vanquished does not mean that the leadership cult must emerge victorious. Democratic citizens may hold the leadership cult in check. Not every corporate manager can be saved from the leadership cult, but everyone who is saved is better fit for democratic leadership.

After all, corporate life has virtues from which democracy could profit. Civility, notable for its absence in the political arena, is a vital part of workaday life in many firms. And only business leaders who understand the leadership cult's immorality are morally qualified to bring those better qualities of corporate life into the democratic political arena.

Perhaps George Bush was one of those who could not have been saved from the leadership cult's considerable appeal to vanity. But it was not written in stone that he had to be president. A better informed citizenry might have recognized his unfitness for democratic leadership.

It shows how desperate is the need for better ethical understanding in our democracy that Bush was able successfully to campaign for president, not once but twice, by presenting himself as a moral leader. He has some good values but, beyond that, has offered little evidence that he understands the importance of professional competence, situational knowledge, and ethical understanding in distinguishing right from wrong. He just seems to believe that he knows in his heart what's right.

Yet we owe it to ourselves to understand Bush a bit better than that. In a morally imperfect world, our leaders will inevitably be impure. But we in the ranks may be better led than otherwise, both practically and morally, if we find the democratic courage to remind those at the head of the file that the cult of moral leadership need not prevail. Although the leadership cult cannot be defeated, it may be held at bay, especially if we teach other leaders that the idea of managing by values has made George Bush not only its proponent but also its patsy.

Acknowledgments

It is a pleasure to express my gratitude to my Babson College colleagues who provided expert assistance from their academic fields or helped in some other way—Kate Buckley, Stephen Collins, Sheila Dinsmoor, Mary Driscoll, Mike Fetters, Bob Halsey, Kandice Hauf, Ross Petty, Cynthia Robinson, Marty Tropp, and Bob Turner. Erik Sirri deserves a special thank you. On the rare occasion when he could not answer one of the many questions I asked him about corporate finance and governance, he found someone who could. The Babson College Board of Research provided a helpful grant at the start of this study.

I wrote part of this book during a year I served as Visiting Frances Willson Thompson Professor of Leadership Studies at Kettering University. For stimulating collegiality I am grateful to Kettering's Department of Liberal Studies and, in particular, Ezekiel Gebissa, Eugene Hynes, Luchen Li, Badrinath Rao, and Hugh Stilley.

George Cotkin, a fellow scholar and faithful friend of many years, read several chapters and offered his usual selfless help. Ross Wolin discussed this book with me for many an evening. Allan Wyatt was an able and generous counselor. John Whitman read parts of an early draft and offered useful suggestions.

Beth Healy of the *Boston Globe* read parts of the manuscript and was able to point the way toward important sources thanks to her investigative reporting on George Bush and Harken Energy. Nat Butler and Yoshi Tsurumi kindly shared their memories of Bush as a Harvard Business School student. Jeff Olson was a helpful and patient editor.

Carol Hoopes, Johanna Hoopes, and Ben Hoopes remain my inspiration.

The ideas and opinions in this book are mine and do not necessarily reflect the views of any of the above people. Responsibility for errors is also mine alone.

Notes

CHAPTER 1: THE LEADERSHIP CULT AND THE MBA PRESIDENT

1. Richard Morin and Dan Balz, "Bush's Popularity Reaches New Low: 58 Percent in Poll Question His Integrity," *Washington Post*, November 4, 2005.

2. Craig Offman, "Bush Campaign Cans Biographer," Salon, available at http://salon.com/books/log/1999/09/27/herskowitz/index.html.

3. Russ Baker, "Why George Went to War," TomPaine.commonsense, available at http:tompaine.com/articles/2005/06/20/why_george_went_to_war.php.

4. *Great Debates in American History*, ed. Marion Mills Miller (New York: Current Literature, 1913), 2:26.

5. Thomas E. Ricks, *Fiasco: The American Military Adventure in Iraq* (New York: Penguin, 2006), 59–60, 64–66.

6. David Knights and Hugh Wilmott, *Introducing Organizational Behaviour and Management* (London: Thomson Learning, 2007), quoted under Leadership at http://www.criticalmanagement.org/teaching/topics.htm.

7. Scott Hennen, "An Oval Office Meeting with President Bush," Hot Talk, available at http://areavoices.com/hottalk/?blog=11130.

8. Kurt Eichenwald, *Conspiracy of Fools: A True Story* (New York: Broadway Books, 2005), 656–57.

9. Eichenwald, *Conspiracy of Fools*, 614.

10. Joe Nocera, "Even at the End, He Didn't Get It," *New York Times*, July 6, 2006.

11. John Chester Miller, *The Wolf by the Ears: Thomas Jefferson and Slavery* (New York: Free Press, 1977), 42.

CHAPTER 2: THE EDUCATION OF A PRESIDENT

1. Bill Minutaglio, *First Son: George W. Bush and the Bush Family Dynasty* (New York: Random House, 1999), 85.

2. Minutaglio, *First Son*, 99.

3. Minutaglio, *First Son*, 121.

4. James Moore, *Bush's War for Reelection: Iraq, the White House, and the People* (Hoboken, NJ: Wiley, 2004), 157.

5. Kit R. Roane, "The Service Question: A Review of President Bush's Guard Years Raises Issues about the Time He Served," September 20, 2004, *U.S. News & World Report*, available at http://www.usnews.com.

6. Moore, *Bush's War*, 167.

7. Glenn W. Smith, *Unfit Commander* (New York: Regan Books, 2004), 25.

8. Smith, *Unfit Commander*, 30.

9. Interview with Yoshi Tsurumi, Baruch College Media, available at http://media.baruch.cuny.edu/faculty/movies/tsurumi_605.mov.

10. The reporter Matthew Cooper has suggested that Romney tackles problems from the other side of the traditional business school dichotomy. Emphasizing analysis rather than gut instinct, Romney "likes his information 'voluminous'" "Please, Not Another M.B.A. President," Portfolio.com. Available at http://www.portfolio.com/careers/features/2007/08/13/Mitt-Romney-MBA#page1.

11. Minutaglio, *First Son*, 157.

12. For a detailed analysis of the shortcomings in the Hawthorne experiment and Harvard professors' mistaken interpretation of it, see James Hoopes, *False Prophets: The Gurus Who Created Modern Management and Why Their Ideas Are Bad for Business Today* (New York: Basic Books, 2003), 146–153.

13. "Hawthorne Experiment Commemorated," *Harbus* (November 15, 1974).

14. Richard Gillespie, *Manufacturing Knowledge* (New York: Cambridge University Press, 1991), 59–64.

15. F. J. Roethlisberger and William J. Dickson, *Management and the Worker* (Cambridge, MA: Harvard University Press, 1967), 553.

16. Abraham Zaleznik, "Managers and Leaders: Are They Different?" *Best of HBR*, January 2004, available at http://tppserver.mit.edu/esd801/psds/11800988_Zaleznik_HBR.pdf.

17. Zaleznik, "Managers and Leaders."

18. Zaleznik, "Managers and Leaders."

19. Zaleznik, "Managers and Leaders."

20. Zaleznik, "Managers and Leaders."

CHAPTER 3: MORAL LEADERSHIP AT HARKEN ENERGY

1. Minutaglio, *First Son*, 205.

2. Minutaglio, *First Son*, 207.

3. Minutaglio, *First Son*, 247.

4. Elizabeth Mitchell, *W: Revenge of the Bush Dynasty* (New York: Berkeley Books, 2000), 261–62.

5. Mitchell, *W*, 263.

6. Thomas Petzinger Jr., Peter Truell, and Jill Abramson, "Family Ties," *Wall Street Journal*, December 6, 1991.

7. Minutaglio, *First Son*, 247.

8. Minutes, Harken Board of Directors, May 11, 1990, from Security and Exchange Commission records published by the Center for Public Integrity, available at http://www.publici.org/search.aspx?strSearch=Harken. Except where otherwise noted, all cited documents pertaining to Bush's career at Harken Energy, his Harken stock sale, and the SEC investigation of Bush are from this source.

9. Minutes, Harken Board of Directors, May 17, 1990.

10. Minutes, Harken Executive Committee, May 8, 1990.

11. Minutes, Special Committee of the Harken Board of Directors, May 17, 1990.

12. Minutes, Harken Board of Directors, May 11, 1990.

13. Minutes, Special Committee of the Harken Board of Directors, May 17, 1990.

14. Minutes, Special Committee of the Harken Board of Directors, May 17, 1990.

15. Mikel D. Faulkner to Harken Energy Corporation Board of Directors, July 13, 1990.

16. Harken Energy Company 10-K Report, 1991, 39.

CHAPTER 4: A MORAL MISTAKE AT HARKEN ENERGY

1. Michael Kranish and Beth Healy, "Board Was Told of Risks before Bush Stock Sale," *Boston Globe*, October 30, 2002.

2. Kranish and Healy, "Board Was Told."

3. Bruce Huff to Edmund Coulson, January 9, 1991.

4. Herbert F. Janick III, Lewis J. Mendelson, James B. Adelman to SEC Files, April 10, 1991.

5. "White House Defends Bush Handling of Stock Sale," CNN.com, July 3, 2002, available at http://archives.cnn.com/2002/ALLPOLITICS/07/03/bush.stock/index.html.

6. Larry Cummings to Bush, October 5, 1989.

7. Herbert F. Janick III, Lewis J. Mendelson, James B. Adelman to SEC Files, April 10, 1991.

8. "Action Memorandum," March 18, 1992.

9. "Action Memorandum," March 18, 1992.

10. Memo to [SEC] File from Herb [Janick] March 17, 1992.

11. Memo to [SEC] File from Herb [Janick], March 17, 1992.

12. Herb Janick, Paul Gerlach, and Jim Adelman to Bruce Hiler, August 21, 1991.

13. "Action Memorandum," March 18, 1992.

14. Minutes, Harken Board of Directors, May 11, 1990.

15. Memo to [SEC] File from Herb [Janick], March 17, 1992.

16. "Confidential Treatment Requested by R. Jordan Pursuant to Letter Dated May 12, 1991."

17. Minutes, Harken Board of Directors, March 14, 1990.

18. Kranish and Healy, "Board Was Told."

19. Herb Janick, Paul Gerlach, and Jim Adelman to Bruce Hiler, August 21, 1991.

20. Kranish and Healy, "Board Was Told."

21. Kranish and Healy, "Board Was Told."

22. "Action Memorandum," March 18, 1992.

23. Lisa Meulbroek to Herb Janick, Lew Mendelson, Jim Adelman, and Paul Gerlach, July 7, 1991.

24. James M. Patell and Mark A. Wolfson, "The Intraday Speed of Adjustment of Stock Prices to Earnings and Dividend Announcements," *Journal of Financial Economics* (June 1984), 228.

25. Meulbroek to Janick, et al., July 7, 1991.

26. Meulbroek to Janick, et al., July 7, 1991.

27. Meulbroek to Janick, et al., July 7, 1991.

28. *CRSP. TS Print.* CD-ROM. University of Chicago, Graduate School of Business; Version 2.60.

29. Faulkner to Harken Board of Directors, August 27, 1990.

30. Michael Kranish, "Bush's Harken Stock Mystery Endures: SEC Filings Point to N.Y. Firm as Possible Purchaser of Shares," *Boston Globe*, November 8, 2002.

CHAPTER 5: THE ETHICS OF LEADERSHIP

1. Niccolò Machiavelli, *The Prince*, trans. and ed. Robert M. Adams (New York: W. W. Norton, 1992), 42.

2. Machiavelli, *The Prince*, 48.

3. Machiavelli, *The Prince*, 42.

4. Machiavelli, *The Prince*, 43.

5. Machiavelli, *The Prince*, 45.

6. Machiavelli, *The Prince*, 46.

7. Machiavelli, *The Prince*, 46.

8. Machiavelli, *The Prince*, 49.

9. Machiavelli, *The Prince*, 49.

10. Aristotle, *Nicomachean Ethics*, trans. F. H. Peters (New York: Barnes and Noble Books, 2004), 25.

11. Immanuel Kant, *Groundwork of the Metaphysics of Morals*, trans. H. J. Paton (New York: Harper Torchbooks, 1964), 88.

12. Kant, *Groundwork*, 71.

13. Kant, *Groundwork*, 96.

14. Jeremy Bentham, *An Introduction to the Principles of Morals and Legislation*, ed. Philip Wheelwright (Doubleday, Doran, & Co.: Garden City, NY, 1935), 9.

15. Ken Blanchard and Michael O'Connor, with Jim Blanchard, *Managing by Values* (San Francisco: Berrett-Koehler, 1997), 54.

16. Blanchard and O'Connor, *Managing by Values*, 45.

17. John Whitman, *Evaluating Philanthropic Foundations: A Comparative Social Values Approach* (Ph.D. Dissertation, University of Toronto, 2006), 5: 1.

18. Blanchard and O'Connor, *Managing by Values*, 112.

19. Blanchard and O'Connor, *Managing by Values*, 20.

20. Blanchard and O'Connor, *Managing by Values*, 44.

21. Blanchard and O'Connor, *Managing by Values*, 65.

22. Blanchard and O'Connor, *Managing by Values*, 88, 86, 94.

23. Blanchard and O'Connor, *Managing by Values*, 79–81.

24. Carolyn B. Thompson and James W. Ware, *The Leadership Genius of George W. Bush: 10 Commonsense Lessons from the Commander in Chief* (Hoboken, NJ: John Wiley & Sons, 2003), 8.

25. Thompson and Ware, *Leadership Genius of George W. Bush*, 11.

CHAPTER 6: CORPORATE SOCIAL IRRESPONSIBILITY

1. Ron Suskind, *The Price of Loyalty: George W. Bush, the White House, and the Education of Paul O'Neill* (New York: Simon & Schuster, 2004), 233.

2. David E. Sanger, "Who Should Mete Out Punishment?" *New York Times*, July 17, 2002.

3. Stephen Labaton, "Bush Seeking Added Rules to Help Protect the Investor," March 8, 2002.

4. Labaton, "Bush Seeking Added Rules."

5. Labaton, "Bush Seeking Added Rules."

6. Elizsabeth Bumiller and Richard A. Oppel, Jr., "Bush Defends Sale of Stock and Vows to Enhance SEC," *New York Times*, July 9, 2002.

7. Transcript of President's Address Calling for New Era of Corporate Integrity," *New York Times*, July 10, 2002.

8. Transcript of President's Address Calling for New Era of Corporate Integrity," *New York Times*, July 10, 2002.

9. Transcript of President's Address Calling for New Era of Corporate Integrity," *New York Times*, July 10, 2002.

10. Floyd Norris, "Taking Hold of the Wheel," *New York Times*, July 16, 2002.

11. Richard A. Oppel, Jr., "In a Shift, Republicans Pledge to Pass Accounting Bill," *New York Times*, July 18, 2002.

12. Richard A. Oppel, Jr., "Little Progress on Corporate Governance Bill," *New York Times*, July 22, 2002.

13. Richard A. Oppel, Jr., "Negotiators Agree on Broad Changes in Business Laws," *New York Times*, July 25, 2002.

14. "Corporate Accountability Reform," The White House, available at http://www.whitehouse.gov/infocus/achievement/chap9.html.

15. Siobhan Hughes, "GAO Seeks Smaller Exemption to Sarbanes-Oxley Provisions," *The Wall Street Journal*, May 9, 2006.

CHAPTER 7: SPIRITUALITY AT WORK

1. Stephen Mansfield, *The Faith of George W. Bush* (New York: Tarcher, 2003), 119.

2. Gilbert W. Fairholm, *Capturing the Heart of Leadership: Spirituality and Community in the New American Workplace* (Westport: Praeger, 2000), 3.

3. Mitchell, *W*, 334.

4. Fairholm, *Capturing the Heart of Leadership*, 8.

5. Ron Suskind, *The Price of Loyalty: George W. Bush, the White House, and the Education of Paul O'Neill* (New York: Simon & Schuster, 2004), 186.

6. *Writings of Charles S. Peirce: A Chronological Edition*, ed. Edward C. Moore et al. (Bloomington: Indiana University Press, 1982–present), 1: 498.

7. Douglas A. Hicks, *Religion and the Workplace: Pluralism, Spirituality, Leadership* (New York: Cambridge University Press, 2003), passim.

8. Hicks, *Religion and the Workplace*, 84.

9. Marvin Olasky, *Compassionate Conservatism* (New York: The Free Press, 2000), 15.

10. "Teen Challenge," *Religion & Ethics NewsWeekly*, Feb. 23, 2001, available at http://www.pbs.org/wnet/religionandethics/week426/cover.html#right.

11. "The Expanding Administrative Presidency: George W. Bush and the Faith-Based Initiative," Roundtable on Religion and Social Welfare Policy, August 2004, available at http://www.ReligionandSocialPolicy.org.

12. "Now," September 26, 2003, available at http://www.pbs.org.

13. "Now," September 26, 2003, available at http://www.pbs.org.

14. David Kuo, *Tempting Faith: An Inside Story of Political Seduction* (New York: Free Press, 2006), 193.

15. Michael Hout and Claude S. Fischer, "Why More Americans Have No Religious Preference: Politics and Generations," *American Sociological Review* (67:2), 165.

CHAPTER 8: THE UNCONSTITUTIONAL WAR ON TERROR

1. Lincoln's critics acknowledged that the Constitution allows for suspension of habeas corpus during a rebellion but argued that the Constitution gave

only Congress, not the president, the right to do it. Craig R. Smith, "Lincoln and Habeas Corpus," available at csulb.edu/~crsmith/lincoln.html.

2. Ivo H. Daalder and James M. Lindsay, *America Unbound: The Bush Revolution in Foreign Policy* (Washington, D.C.: Brookings Institution Press, 2003), 78.

3. Bob Woodward, *Bush at War* (New York: Simon & Schuster, 2002), 15.

4. Suskind, *Price of Loyalty*, 184.

5. Jennifer Elsea, "Terrorism and the Law of War: Trying Terrorists as War Criminals before Military Commissions," Congressional Research Service, The Library of Congress, Updated December 11, 2001, 13.

6. Elsea, "Terrorism and the Law of War," 12–13.

7. Richard W. Stevenson, "President Makes it Clear: Phrase is 'War on Terror,'" *New York Times*, August 4, 2005.

8. Eric Alterman and Mark Green, *The Book on Bush: How George W. Bush (Mis)leads America* (New York: Viking, 2004), 234.

9. Laurence Wright, *The Looming Tower: Al Qaeda and the Road to 9/11* (New York: Knopf, 2006), 259–60.

10. Katharine Q. Seelye and Elisabeth Bumiller, "Bush Labels Aerial Terrorist Attacks 'Acts of War,'" *New York Times*, September 13, 2001.

11. Michael Novak, "Good, Evil, and My Friend Irwin: A Literary Luncheon with President Bush," *The Daily Standard*, March 14, 2007.

12. Mary Parker Follett, *The New State: Group Organization the Solution of Popular Government* (New York: Longmans, Green, 1918), 357–58.

13. Bob Woodward, *Plan of Attack* (New York: Simon & Schuster, 2004), 26.

14. Woodward, *Plan of Attack*, 81.

15. Susan Milligan, "Congress Gives Bush Power to Hunt Terrorists," *Boston Globe*, September 15, 2001.

16. Ricks, *Fiasco*, 52.

17. Ricks, *Fiasco*, 52.

18. Ricks, *Fiasco*, 378.

19. Ron Suskind, *The One Percent Doctrine: Deep Inside America's Pursuit of Its Enemies Since 9/11* (New York: Simon & Schuster, 2006), 123.

20. Ron Suskind, "Without a Doubt," *New York Times*, October 17, 2004.

21. Suskind, *One Percent Doctrine*, 225.

22. Woodward, *State of Denial*, 260.

23. Rajiv Chandrasekaran, *Imperial Life in the Emerald City: Inside Iraq's Green Zone* (New York: Knopf, 2006), 161.

24. L. Paul Bremer, *My Year in Iraq: The Struggle to Build a Future of Hope* (New York: Simon & Schuster, 2006), 8.

25. Chandrasekaran, *Imperial Life*, 91.

26. Chandrasekaran, *Imperial Life*, 99.

27. Charles Hoskinson, "Bush: I Would Do It Again," *Sydney Morning Herald*, July 11, 2004.

28. Nir Rosen, "The Flight from Iraq," *New York Times*, May 13, 2007.

29. "Bush: Iraqi Democracy Making Progress," CNN, Dec. 12, 2005, available at cnn.com.

30. Gilbert Burnham, Riyadh Lafta, Shannon Doocy, Les Roberts, "Mortality After the 2003 Invasion of Iraq: A Cross-Sectional Cluster Sample Survey," *The Lancet*, October 11, 2006, available at http://www.thelancet.com/webfiles/images/journals/lancet/s0140673606694919.pdf.

CONCLUSION: EARN MORAL INFLUENCE, DON'T USE IT

1. Max Weber, *The Theory of Social and Economic Organization*, tr. A. M. Henderson and Talcott Parsons (New York: Free Press, 1947), 358.

2. Weber, *Theory of Social and Economic Organization*, 359.

3. Weber, *Theory of Social and Economic Organization*, 360.

Index

About the Author

JAMES HOOPES is the Murata Professor of Business Ethics at Babson College. He is the author of *False Prophets: The Gurus Who Created Modern Management and Why Their Ideas Are Bad for Business Today.* He is regularly quoted on business-and-society issues in the *New York Times, BusinessWeek,* and *USA Today.*